SCENE CHANGES IN KASHMIR, INDIA AND PAKISTAN

SCENE CHANGES IN KASHMIR, INDIA AND PAKISTAN

PRAN CHOPRA

GYAN PUBLISHING HOUSE
NEW DELHI-110002

Scene Changes in Kashmir, India and Pakistan
(International Relation, Political Science)

Rs. 540

ISBN: 81-212-0834-3

Published in 2003 in India by
Gyan Publishing House
5, Ansari Road, Darya Ganj, New Delhi-110002
Phones : 23282060, 23261060, Fax : 011-23285914
E-mail : gyanbook@vsnl.com
Website : http://www.gyanbooks.com

Laser Typesetting at : Shree Vaishnavi Creations, New Delhi
Printed at : Print Perfect, New Delhi-110 064

*Dedicated to my years in
Lahore, 1921-1944*

Contents

Part III : Surrounding Scenarios

Introduction

The Old and the New

No act of man and few acts of nature have caused such a deep and widespread tragedy in so short a period of time, and have proved to be so destructive of the lives and happiness of so many millions of people, as the partition of India in August 1947. No assessment of the benefits of British rule over India or the damage it inflicted on the country can be complete without fully taking account this dark hour of Indian history.

The darkest part of this hour is the tragedy of the state of Jammu and Kashmir, a priceless pearl of the natural and cultural beauty of India, which has been tortured by war and terror for more than 50 years now, because of international intrigues and rival claims on Kashmir by the two new states of India and Pakistan which were created by the Indian Independence Act passed by the British Parliament.

This Act is remembered in both countries as the Partition Act because it divided the former single India into two countries, and plunged both countries and the state into this half a century old war. The result does no credit to the sagacity of the people of India or Pakistan, or to the wisdom or motives of Great Britain, or to the standards of fair play or foresight of the big - none of them great - powers retain which for their own shortsighted reasons manoeuvered the state and the whole subcontinent into this tragedy.

The same Act of the British Parliament which had

created Pakistan had given to the ruler of each of the hundreds of "princely" states, sort of British protectorates, the right to decide whether he would like to join India or Pakistan or opt for independence. While the ruler of Jammu and Kashmir was still weighing his options Pakistan launched a surprise attack on the state and captured a large slice of its western districts. India could do little about it because the state had not acceded to it. But when Pakistani forces reached the state's capital, Srinagar, the ruler asked for and was granted accession to India.

With only the Srinagar airfield still left as link, and that too within range of enemy guns, India organised one of the most daring airlifts in military history and not only saved the airport and the city but began a counter-attack. But after pushing them a safe enough distance away, and well enough able now to clear them out of the whole state, India decided that instead of pursuing the war it would pursue peace and would take the matter to the United Nations as an aggrieved victim of aggression. But this decision proved to be more commendable for the honourable motivation of those who took it than for the quality of political judgement displayed by them. They had failed to understand that, coveting the usefulness of the strategic location of Kashmir, the western powers which had already gained control of the United Nations would exploit the case to the hilt for serving their cold war aims.

This failure on India's part gave a powerful advantage to Pakistan, an ally of these powers, and it inflicted a severe disadvantage upon India which they all regarded as a hidden ally of their enemy in the cold war, the Soviet Union. For half a century they shielded Pakistan against the well proven Indian charge that in the process of gaining its own independence Pakistan had denied to the ruler of Jammu and Kashmir the right given to him by the departing British : to choose, in peace, between India, Pakistan, and independence. Instead they tried to use the United Nations to force India to accept what the United Nations itself had denied to everyone by ruling, thrice, that no right of self-determination belonged to any territory which by law had become a legitimate part of another country.

In the course of time the debates in the United Nations came to be used for falsely pillorying India for defying UN resolutions, although it was India which had accepted them and it was Pakistan which had stymied them by refusing to carry out the conditions stipulated in them for implementing them. UN's own representatives later recorded the conclusion that the resolutions had been obstructed for so long that it was no longer practicable to implement them. But the political managers of the UN debates continued to use them for their own political purposes which India had failed to foresee.

It was in the midst of this sense of despondency over diplomacy that India and the state of Jammu and Kashmir had to start facing a new and more concrete threat to their internal and external security. India had done well enough in coping with Pakistan's direct military threat, not only in throwing back Pakistan's army and the raiders openly backed by that army in 1947-48, but also in defeating a more blatant, open, organised and determined bid by the whole Pakistan army in 1965. In 1971, India routed the Pakistan army in the Bangladesh war. But from the late 1980s India became one of the first countries to face a more insidious and more dangerous enemy, a covert form of war through fanatical terrorists, the jehadies, who fought in the name of a fundamentalist form of Islam. In other contexts they are often described as "non-state" actors but in this case they were clearly serving the ambition of the state of Pakistan to capture Kashmir since it had faced only defeat in all regular wars with India.

What has been happening for half a century to India and Pakistan at the hands of each other, and to the state at the hands both and the puppets nurtured by each, is a tale that has been told often. So is the tale of cynical exploitation of the situation by the big powers in and outside the United Nations, and what that has done to the UN itself. The repeated telling of it has only confirmed the impression in the minds of many that the whole of the Indian sub-continent, and with it the state of Jammu and Kashmir, are caught in a tragic stalemate from which there is no escape.

What is relatively new and bears repeating, however, is that a number of factors, some indigenous to Kashmir, to India and to Pakistan, some close to the sub-continent and others in distant countries, have combined to create some movement in a stalemate which had appeared to be relentless and open to resolution only by military force. It is ironic but true that violence itself played a part in creating this movement because its failure in the various new forms in which Pakistan tried it might have convinced Pakistan more than earlier events had done that the new forms of violence would not work any more than the older forms had done.

The biggest new form tried by Pakistan, in Kargil in 1999-2000, was an updated version of the first ever form tried by it, in 1947-48 : a combination of irregular forces for creating a surprise, a diversion and softening up the front, followed by the regular army delivering the punch. While one of Pakistan's few civilian and elected Prime Ministers, Nawaz Sharrif, and the Indian Prime Minister, Mr Vajpayee, were working out an extensive and solid programme of peaceful cooperation between the two countries, and signing on what became famous as the Lahore documents of 1999, the Chief of the Army Staff of Pakistan, General Parvez Musharraf, who was soon to stage a military coup and become Pakistan's fifth military dictator, was busy sending armed irregulars to Kargil, a mountain range dominating a very sensitive stretch of the only road linking Srinagar with Ladakh, the largest province of the state and adjacent to Tibet on one side and the outreach of Soviet Central Asia on another. Believing that the time and ground situations were now ripe, Musharraf now played his army card. But here again Indian army and air force took innovative and daring actions to frustrate Pakistan.

In December of the following year Pakistan made its boldest moves with the jehadi card. Perhaps the handlers of Pakistan's terrorists recalled that tragedy in Burma in the late 1940s when just a few armed attackers broke into the country's Parliament when it was in session in Rangoon and shot the whole cabinet dead, including the father of Aung San Syu Kyi, General Aung San, whom I came to know in Burma in 1944-45 as the most shy of all generals I ever met.

But whatever their inspiration, the managers of the jehad in India planned a similar attack on Parliament in Delhi at a time when most ministers are expected to be in their seats, clearly within sight and reach from many of the galleries of the House. A band of guerrillas rushed at the building and had reached within a shot of success when all of them were killed, one by one, by the security police. Their operation was much bolder than that of another band which massacred scores of worshippers at a temple in Gujarat, perhaps to provoke a communal conflagration.

But the pain of the most sustained and merciless part of the jehad has been borne by the people of Kashmir. Ever since the late 1980s a determined campaign, masterminded from within Pakistan, has been carried out there to terrorise all those who support the state's continued accession to India, and to drive a wedge between the Muslims and non-Muslims of the state. The great majority of those dozens of thousands of Kashmiris who have been killed by the terrorists or by the security forces were Muslims. But that has made no difference to the main motive of the campaign of the terrorists, to get Kashmir for Pakistan.

But over the past seven years or so the tide has been turning against the terrorist campaign. It had failed even earlier in gaining the support of the majority of the people, except of those Muslims who subscribed to the religious fanaticism of the terrorists, many of them heavily Talibanised by now. But a few years ago it began to lose the support of the freedom activists as well because of its blind obedience to Pakistan and its attempt to impose fanatical Islam upon the gentler Islam of the sufi faith of Kashmiri

Hindus and Muslims alike. At the same time Pakistan itself began to lose the support it had earlier received from many influential countries of the west for cold war reasons, because that war itself came to an end. Musharraf's actions in denouncing the Lahore agreements and once again putting Pakistan under military rule further dampened the interest of democratic elements in the west.

There was some re-kindling of this interest for a time because of the expectation that Musharraf would ardently support western actions in the predominantly Islamic part of the world. But that did not happen, and even to the extent it did it only lent force to the opposition he faced from Islamic fundamentalists within Pakistan, who began to capture important political positions in Pakistan. On the other hand many countries began to wonder whether they would be the gainers or losers if they were seen by the world as habitual supporters of a retrograde Pakistan and opponents of a democratic and economically progressive India.

It is possible that some future event or crisis, for example a sudden eruption in Afghanistan or a renewed flareup between Iran and America, might send Washington scurrying for support and Pakistan might be one of its destinations. But while this possibility was a strong asset for Pakistan once it has ceased to be so. As has been discussed at greater length later in this book, Pakistan has lost much of the advantage it once had because of its strategic location in the Islamic world. This has happened for three reasons.

First, it has ceased to be a leader in the Islamic world, as it once was. Should Musharraf or his successors try to regain that position by embracing Islamic fundamentalism they will, in the first place, find that this space has been occupied already by the genuinely fundamentalist parties in Pakistan whom the country's "establishment" cannot outbid; and in the second place Pakistan will then cease to be a destination much favoured by Washington except in a hostile sense. Second, Pakistan no longer enjoys the advantage of contiguity with sensitive areas like Afghanistan because that space too has been occupied by others. Third, America no longer needs Pakistani space as a bridge to Islamic Central Asia because America has its own bases there all over the place. Such leverage as Pakistan may yet have will be heavily off-set by domestic reactions in America and in Pakistan to the company they keep.

This turning of the tide is the theme of this book. It has been argued out in three sections. In the first section, "Still Frames", are extensive overviews of South Asia or of India, Pakistan, and Kashmir, taken at junctures of special opportunity or timeliness. In the second section, "The Moving Picture", there are a succession of quick assessments, kind of snapshots, of specific aspects of the South Asia scene, particularly in Kashmir, the rest of India, and Pakistan. In the third section there are similar assessments of more distant situations which, however, are of relevance to developments in South Asia. The periods of time when the assessments were made have been indicated, to show the pace of the change. Between them they make a picture of rapidly changing situations.

Most of these assessments have been published by others in different places. They are used here with grateful acknowledgement to them. Special thanks are due to *The Hindu* newspaper because more of these assessments were first published there than anywhere else. Because these snapshots were taken and published at different points of time, a few overlaps and repetitions had to be tolerated to complete the meaning in each new context.

PART-I
STILL FRAMES

Introduction

Shifting Perspectives

All through the decades of the cold war Pakistan had an inestimable asset in the eyes of the most powerful members of the anti-communist alliance, its strategic location on the softest flanks of the Soviet Union and China. This western perception of the strategic value of Pakistan was exploited to the hilt by all the rulers of Pakistan in the first four decades of its history, and by none more than by General Zia-ul-Haq, in whose eyes this became the material for building a new destiny for the country. But gradually this asset expired as the cold war drew to an end. What was left in its place was a country which was being hollowed out from within by its closest friends because, whether with their eyes open or shut, they only used it as a base for their strategic operations. They did not see it as a nation which needed to be helped in building itself up as nations are built. This, and the consequent Talibanisation of Pakistan, are the theme of the first paper.

The second paper takes the theme further by contrasting the electoral experiences of India and Pakistan and of the state of Jammu and Kashmir. The contrast is instructive because it shows the role of legitimate politics in the building of a viable society and polity, and what harm the absence or subversion of this role can do. Particularly instructive is the role of legitimate electoral politics in Kashmir and its effect upon the state's place in India. The role was strong and the place was of honourable prominence in the years when the people of the state were free to elect governments of their choice by their free will. Both the role and the place plummeted when the electoral process began to be subverted. But the scene changed overnight when that legitimacy was restored, and with it came more improvement and better law and order than could be achieved by authoritarian methods alone. The contrast with the electoral process in Pakistan could not have been more instructive.

The third paper was written in the year 2,000, soon after the time when "the Lahore process" was disrupted by the Kargil war, and before the time when "the healing touch" election in Kashmir began to help in reviving it. This paper thus presents an overview which can be the bench mark for what has been happening since then in the internal developments in the state and in India as a whole, and in the relations of both was Pakistan.

1

Pakistan Loses a Strategic Advantage

It is generally assumed, and history confirms, that the geography of a country is the most durable factor in the shaping of its overall strategies, whether foreign, domestic, political, economic, or security. Its geography determines how much of it is mountain, desert, coastal, riverine, cultivated or barren; how much of its population is agricultural, industrial, seafaring, tribal, nomadic, pastoral. These in turn are the pillars on which rests its civilisation, society, politics. And its capabilities, in war and peace, which ultimately must shape its strategies. A country's geography, and therefore the factors derived from it, changes significantly only if the country gains or loses territory. That may happen only rarely. But when it does its impact is great and quick, as Pakistan knows from its own direct experience.

Pakistan could pose a direct military threat to vital territories of India from its eastern wing until 1971, and thus constantly expose India to a military challenge on two fronts simultaneously. But in that crucial year it lost that capability for ever. The subversive intrusions it could still engineer through Bangladesh were negligible compared to the military assault it could have mounted earlier. Such a change can mean much to a country which does not have many chips to bargain with as much as it can with the lie of its frontiers.

> **Pakistan's experience has confirmed that a country's borders can be a boon to it, because Pakistan has been extracting a huge bonanza from its geographical location and boundaries. But now they are becoming a burden.**
>
> **Thoughtful Pakistanis have been feeling of late that the country might have been better off today if, in the past, its geography had not so powerfully determined its priorities in so many spheres of its future as a nation. What will they be thinking and feeling tomorrow as they see how Pakistan's priorities have undermined its aims ?**
>
> **I am going to argue that whereas at one time Pakistan's geographical location and the resulting contiguities conferred considerable strategic advantages on the country, now they have ceased to do so. In fact they can become an embarrassment if Pakistan does not quickly put its house in order.**
>
> **This is because Pakistan' borders do not satisfy any of the three criteria on which the usefulness of the borders of any country depends. First, that the country should have complete control over its own side of the borders. Second, it should have friendly relations with the countries on the other side. Third, it should be stronger than the neighbour.**

At its birth Pakistan was a geographical anomaly, a country of two halves separated by nearly two thousand miles of another country towards which, from its inception, it was hostile and with which it began its relations with a war. This was bound to become an unsustainable anomaly as Bangladesh, located in a very different geographical environment from that of West Pakistan, developed a different ethos and polity, one which inclined it more and towards democracy in a more or less secular mode. Friction with the very different ethos of West Pakistan developed within the first decade of the existence of Pakistan. During the second decade it festered into conditions of near war between the two wings. Pakistan survived this oddity for some time, in a manner of speaking, but mainly because West Pakistan was able to impose upon East Pakistan the geo-strategic determinants of its own foreign and domestic policies which it had inherited from its own location at the edge of the West Asian Islamic world.

These determinants had converted Pakistan into a convenient (and lucrative) launching pad for the cold war strategies of one super power, the United States, against the other, the Soviet Union, in the Middle East and Central Asia. Pakistan had its obvious geo-strategic attractions for the United States. Its hostility towards India, which was seen as an ally of Soviet Union, was rightly seen by the United States as a good starting point for persuading Pakistan to join American strategies. It is true that Pakistan was only a pawn in American games in those days, not the player that it was to try to become in the 1980s. But even as a pawn it was able to put its territory out on a very profitable rent for those games, picking up a rentier's gains with one hand and with the other receiving America's powerful backing against India on the Kashmir issue. This was the beginning of a phase in which all of Pakistan's geo-strategic advantages were joined in synergy in reinforcing each other. This phase was to peak in the 1980s.

In the American view Pakistan, a country that had just come into being on the strength of its appeal to the Muslim majority in Pakistan, would be a good companion to display to the predominantly Islamic peoples of the Middle East as America lined them up against the "godless communists." More important, America could put to its own diplomatic uses such affinities as Pakistan already had with the large Muslim bulk in Soviet Central Asia, Iran and Afghanistan, thanks to the ties of Islam which Pakistan had with the populace of these countries, and the historical links it had with many Islamic power elites in this area, going back to the days of the Muslim dynasties which had ruled over India for close upon a thousand years.

But most important for America was the advantage of geography which Pakistan offered to it for convenient access to the Muslims of southern Soviet Union and western China for such use as they could be in the ideological aspects of America's future tussles with these two leaders of the communist world. This was the biggest single determinant that the geography of West Pakistan imposed upon the security and foreign policy priorities of Pakistan as a whole even though one half of it, that is East Pakistan, had no great stake in them. Pakistan was also able to use its geographical location to advantage in winning China's support against India in the wake of the rift which grew between India and China over the northernmost territories of Jammu and Kashmir which Pakistan had captured during its earlier attacks on Kashmir. Pakistan gifted away a slice of this territory to China to enable the latter to build a valuable link between western China and the Arabian Sea, which was among China's priorities.

The second great determinant, even more compelling in the immediate context than the first, was imposed upon the country as a whole by the contiguity of West Pakistan with Kashmir, which Pakistan claimed on the ground that the majority of the people of Jammu and Kashmir were Muslims and its territory was contiguous to West Pakistan, and therefore the state must be taken away from India and joined to Pakistan. Here again East Pakistan, being more than a couple of thousand miles from Kashmir, had much less of a commitment to this determinant than West Pakistan had. But taken together these two factors, its claim on Kashmir and its usefulness to America, set the whole of Pakistan on a pre-determined course in foreign and security policies.

Or did so until East Pakistan drifted away in a manner which was to change the shape of Pakistan beyond recognition. So long as Pakistan had one wing for use against India in the west and another in the east, it could threaten India from both sides, insidiously through migrations, and militarily when it dared to do so. But when East Pakistan became the independent Bangladesh, Pakistan lost much of this advantage, as discussed in detail in the present author's books, *India's Second Liberation* and *The Challenge of Bangladesh*. Until then, the two geo-strategic determinants of the two-winged Pakistan shaped not only its external aims but also the domestic polity of the country as a whole and of each wing separately.

Since America's interests in Pakistan were primarily of a military nature it invested its political and military influence almost entirely in the armed forces. Although claiming to be a champion of democracy, America mistrusted the political process and political parties in Pakistan, fearing what the policies of the country might be if the people were allowed to choose their government freely. This was partly for the reason that democracy was as yet unstable in Pakistan as a whole, but mainly for the reason that the more populous eastern wing, which would count for more in a genuine election, was much less sympathetic to the American project of keeping the military in power in Pakistan so that the country may be used as an American bridgehead with the Middle East and as an American spring board against communist power in Asia.

Given the influence which American power and patronage had in the politics and the economy of Pakistan, its preference for the western wing and for the military elite within that wing tilted the whole political and economic structure of Pakistan in favour of the western wing and the armed forces there. This tilt was to have a much more profound influence on the politics, geography, and geo-strategic future of South Asia than the more famous tilt of the American President, Richard Nixon, in favour of Pakistan during the war in 1971 which was to break Pakistan into two. An attendant consequence was that to the (limited) extent that electoral processes were allowed in Pakistan they could be exploited only by a socio-political ally of the military, namely the feudal landed aristocracy of the western wing.

This further widened the rift between the two wings, because the eastern wing had been much more active in democratic politics under the leadership of the Awami League and its left-inclined leader, Sheikh Mujib. As this difference between the two wings became sharper, the army-based political elite in the western wing tried even harder to deny the Awami League its due share of political power in the eastern wing and to deny the eastern wing its due share power in the country as a whole. This led to intense political agitation in the eastern wing and its brutal suppression by the military backed government there. As the crisis became deeper, and as a tool against the more or less secular politics of the Awami League, the army unleashed a communal wave by launching genocidal attacks on the large Hindu minority in the eastern wing.

This sucked India into the inter-wing war of Pakistan as several millions of Hindus fled into India. The Indian army intervened to stem this tide, and in the war which ensued the eastern wing proclaimed its independence and became Bangladesh, which broke Jinnah's proud achievement into two. Pakistan blamed India for the break up, and revenge became the driving force of its policies. But, what is more important, it also began a phase in which the internal frontiers of Pakistan, that is the relations between the different provinces of Pakistan and the relations of each of them with the central government in Islamabad began to compete with its external frontiers for the attention of the country.

No tragedy could have been worse for Pakistan, and no start could have been worse for the relations between India and the single wing country that Pakistan now became. But a consequence which took longer to unfold was a reversal of the role of Pakistan's borders in the geo-politics of the country, and in the shaping of its domestic politics, its foreign policy, and its overall viability. Hitherto Pakistan's geographical location had been triggering one factor after another in its external relations which, taken together, enabled the government of Pakistan to milk its relations with America to the maximum in terms of money, military sinews, political favours for the government and for key individuals, and most of all by way of western support for its baseless case on Kashmir. This was to continue for another decade or so.

But after that a reverse phase began during which Pakistan's borders began to exert baleful influences on the welfare of the country, with each influence aggravating the others and all of them together pushing the country towards becoming what some American analysts were to call it later, " a failed state." But before getting into that, a brief comment on a related but different theme. It concerns the most promising years in the history of Pakistan which, unfortunately, also became its most tragic years before they could deliver on their promise.

It has often been argued that there is something about Islam which makes Islamic countries impervious to democracy. The argument gains credibility from the fact that so many of the Muslim majority countries have undemocratic governments. But Pakistan, perhaps the first country to claim that it came into being on the basis of the Islamic identity of its people, and also perhaps the first to eliminate so brutally such a large proportion of its non-Muslim population, also had some interludes which show that a Muslim country is not necessarily averse to democracy, and whether in fact it becomes democratic or not depends on its political experiences and fortunes, not on the religion of its people.

Before what became Pakistan was separated from what was till then India, it partook of the freedom struggle waged by Gandhi and his stalwart followers, like Abdul Ghaffar Khan and his brother, Dr. Khan Saheb, in the North-West Frontier Province; G.M. Sayed in Sind; and a number of other Muslim and non-Muslim political leaders in all the provinces of what was to become West Pakistan, and such non-feudal leaders in East Bengal and Calcutta as Suhrawardy and peasant leaders like Fazalul Haq. The Pakistan movement as a whole had also been led by such suave and city-bred leaders as Jinnah and Liaquat Ali Khan. Therefore, Pakistan had little difficulty in starting on a democratic foot, and might have continued on that path but for the deaths of Jinnah and Liaquat Ali in quick succession, and the toll taken among other leaders of that kind by the intrigues and coups which followed the two deaths. In India too, Gandhi and Patel had died in quick succession, but there was not only Nehru who was still around; there was a whole galaxy of regional leaders who had matured in the course of the freedom struggle, and a party, the Congress, which also had come to manhood during the same struggle. But something very different happened in Pakistan.

The army took over in Pakistan, not a new generation of political leaders. That did not happen because Pakistan had a large Muslim population but because all its policies had became a hostage to one single objective, how to get Kashmir. If that involved subjecting Pakistan's polity to Pakistan's military, so be it. That was not considered to be too heavy a price to pay for American support on Kashmir, and if Pakistan's military said it could get that support only if Pakistan fitted itself into America's military projects, then that was all right too.

After the death of its founding leaders, Pakistan as well as some of its provinces went through long spells of various kinds of authoritarian rule under a succession of civilian leaders, and then moved deeper into direct military rule, first under General Mirza and then, for many years, under Generals Ayub Khan and Yahya Khan. And yet, under a dynamic leader, Zulfikar Ali Bhutto, who had been building his base in civilian and elective politics in the face of the opposition of the army and various feudal chieftains, Pakistan moved into constitutional democracy of the parliamentary variety. It also adopted a constitution which was in some ways more democratic than the one India had at that time. The same thing happened again when Zulfikar's daughter, Benazir Bhutto, once a prominent member of the Oxford Union in Britain, began to follow in her father's footsteps despite the long spell of military and strictly Islamist rule imposed on Pakistan by General Zia, who had first deposed and then hanged her father.

It is not implied here that the kind of democracy Pakistan had for various spells under Jinnah-Liaquat Ali or under Bhutto or Benazir or under her electoral rival, Nawaz Sharrif, who too was to deposed by a military man, General Musharraf, had a great deal in common with the more genuine democracy which many countries have known even in this part of the world. The limited point here is only that whether a country moves towards democracy or not is not determined so much by whether its population consists mostly of Muslims or not, but by what its society's experience of politics has been through much of its history. It is true that this experience has been missed by most of the Muslim majority countries. But the reasons for this lie elsewhere than in the religion professed by their peoples.

Islam has little to do with the reasons why Islamic West Pakistan subjected the more numerous Islamic people of

East Pakistan to a barbaric dictatorship or why the Islamist General Zia had to hang Bhutto or why General Musharraf, who began his reign by trying to prove that he was not very orthodox, had to depose and send into exile Prime Minister Nawaz Sharrif, who still had a large majority behind him in the National Assembly. All that flowed directly from two causes : first, the distortion of Pakistan's overall personality by the implacable ambition to get Kashmir; and the room that individual intrigues and rivalries found in the absence of institutions and a broader range of policies.

But to return to the influence of its borders on the policies and viability of Pakistan. The first three military dictators, Generals Mirza, Ayub, and Yahya Khan, had only a single window vision, focussed on Kashmir (plus of course the preservation of their own and the military's hold on power). They had only marginal interest in strategic aims beyond the country's borders, or even in domestic polity, except for General Ayub's flirtation with "basic democracies". But a different chapter began with General Zia, a person of Indian origin. First of all, he was the most ambitious on behalf of Islam. He not only tried harder than any of his predecessors – or successors , so far – to impose Quranic laws on Pakistan. He also had a vision of establishing an Islamic empire which would not only extend from India in the east to Iran in the west, would not only include the whole of neighbouring Afghanistan, but would also extend in the north-west right up to the heart of Central Asia where the Islamic regions of the Soviet Union ended and the Russian regions began. But what fuelled his ambition was not Islamic fervour so much as two more or less secular developments.

In my view it is plausible that he realised, more than any other Pakistani ruler before him, that Pakistan would not get Kashmir by continuing to wage war upon India. On the other hand the instability resulting from further wars for Kashmir might only further inflame wars between Islamic sects within Pakistan, such as the bloody clashes between

Sunnis and Shias, which were getting bloodier and more frequent. (One theory about Zia's hitherto unexplained death in an air crash has it that the Shia pilot of the plane deliberately crashed it in revenge for the death of a prominent Shia leader in just such a crash.) Secondly, and simultaneously, he became engrossed in a much more promising possibility that he saw opening up on the opposite side from Kashmir, in Afghanistan.

Military strategists in Pakistan have always looked with longing upon the vast open spaces of Afghanistan, hoping to acquire sufficient influence in that country to be able to use it as "strategic depth" in the hinterland of Pakistan if a clash with India went wrong. In geographical terms the hope was not unrealistic but it was overturned by history and by the wrong strategies Pakistan followed in pursuit of this aim. History has bound Afghanistan for centuries to what was to become Pakistan, and where history left off demography took over. The plains of Afghanistan and Pakistan were always stepping stones for the ambitions of invaders as they looked with the longing eyes at the wealth of the plains of northern India, whether they came from west of Afghanistan, like the Greeks, Scythians, and Persians, or from Afghanistan itself like the Ghaznies and Lodhis, or from the north-west of Afghanistan, like the Moghuls. The most famous among the Mughals, Babar, gave a wistful expression to this vision when he said that if he divided his conquests among his sons he would give the Indian plains to one son, the plains which became Pakistan to another, but would keep Kabul for himself because from there he could keep one eye on his conquests to the south-east, that is up to the Ganges, but also keep the other eye on Ferghana, in the north-west, the little principality in present day Uzbekistan from where, as a boy-king, he had been driven out by an uncle and where he hoped to return one day. But he was to die in Kabul.

To these linkages between Pakistan and Afghanistan,

another was added by the Pathans, a highly distinctive and assertive collection of tribes who are in majority in Afghanistan and form most of the population of the neighbouring Pakistan province of North-West Frontier Province. This ethnic bridge, now strengthened by a newly awakened sense of Islamic unity between the two sides of the Afghan-Pakistan border, had been earlier used by invaders coming into India whether, from Afghanistan or lands further to the west. They recruited warlike levies as they marched through Afghanistan into India. The rulers of present day Pakistan did not require much imagination to see that there might be a chance here one day to use this bridge in the reverse direction. They saw Pakistan as militarily the most organised Muslim majority country between Indonesia in South-East Asia and Turkey in Europe, the most patronised by the wealth and power of America in its war against the Soviet Union, and best able to deploy the space, the peoples, the Islamic zeal of neighbouring Afghanistan as a base for mounting an assault on the Central Asian citadel of communism.

General Zia, the last military ruler of Pakistan before the present one, General Musharraf, must have become acutely conscious of the emerging need for these advantages as he saw the same communists taking a firm foothold in Afghanistan, first in the form of Afghanistan's own leftist parties and then as the Soviet army. He aimed to counter this with his own agenda of "Nizam-e-Mustafa" for converting Pakistan, hitherto a reasonably modern minded Muslim majority state, into a country and a society ruled in every way by the edicts of Islam, confronting a Sovietised Afghanistan and Central Asia on one side and on the other side a Hindu majority India which was always better known as "Hindoostan" in the lands north and west of Pakistan. Perhaps perception of this opportunity was made sharper in Zia's days by a growing realisation that Pakistan would never win militarily against India and it should try the tactics of subversion by holding up the attractions of Islamic zeal before the Muslim population of India, the second largest in the world, and the only Muslim majority state in India, Jammu and Kashmir. They might see their own faces in the mirror of an Islamised Pakistan.

As Zia's strategy developed, the two parts of it became fused into a single whole, that is to calm down on the border with India, and even on Kashmir to some extent, and thereby free the energies of Pakistan first for a push into Afghanistan and then from there farther into Central Asia. This is what shaped his earliest steps, which were to lead later to the Talibanisation of Afghanistan. First, Pakistan cultivated American support for subversive actions against the Soviet backed regime in Afghanistan. Second, it enlarged the subversion beyond individual steps of sabotage or skirmishes, to the development of an alternative polity and government, and an alternative military power in Afghanistan, manned by Afghans but led and directed by the Pakistan armed forces. Third, it ensured a dominant position in this structure for Pushtoon Afghans through Zia's most favoured Afghan, Hekmatyar, with non-Pushtoon elements also brought into it through the rebel Afghan alliance, patronised by Zia, between Hekmatyar and Shia, Uzbek, Tajik and other elements. Fourth, it made room for Pakistan's efforts to lure India into a "no-war pact", which would freeze the capabilities of India's superior armed forces but leave Pakistan free to raise or lower the temperature of subversion in Kashmir as circumstances may allow. Fifth, through the sharper profile of Pakistan as an Islamist state, it acquired a more elevated place in the comity of Islamic nations which had been gaining an important place in international affairs and the United Nations since the oil shock of the early 1970s.

Hence General Zia's first gambit. As soon as Soviet forces invaded Afghanistan, the Indian Prime Minister of the day, Mrs Gandhi, sent her Foreign Minister (and later Prime Minister) Mr Narsimha Rao, to Pakistan with a two-fold mission, to assure Pakistan that India would not take any advantage of the new situation at the expense of Pakistan, and second, to consult how the two countries may jointly deal with the situation. Mr Rao first conveyed these messages in private, and later announced them at a public lecture which the Indian Consul-General in Karachi managed to arrange for him. Pakistan's reaction, conveyed in private, was that India should first cut its forces on the Indo-Pakistan border by half. India rightly saw this as a move by General Zia to free himself for whatever he might wish to do in the west, in Afghanistan and beyond.

From that time on, Pakistan's geographical location became potentially a more strategic asset for it than it had ever been before. Till then, it had only been an asset Pakistan could make available to others and for doing so earn such goodwill and gifts as it could. Now Zia evolved a vision in which Pakistan would use the asset on its own behalf by enlarging its place significantly in a very significant region. Whether this was or was not too ambitious a vision to be acceptable to Pakistan's superiors is a matter of opinion. But it is not without meaning that among those who speculated about the causes of the plane crash which killed Zia, there were not only some who related it to the bitter rivalries between Pakistan's Shias and Sunnis but also some who thought his ambitions on behalf of Pakistan had become inconvenient for those who wanted to use Pakistan for more limited purposes. Among those who thought the latter explanation was more plausible was a young military aid to President Zia who put in his papers soon after the crash. But however plausible or otherwise these speculations might be, it remains a fact that after General Zia's death Pakistan's importance went on declining in the eyes of its allies, and perhaps in its own eyes as well.

Within just a few years of the death of General Zia, Pakistan began to lose the leverage it had acquired in its international relations because of its strategic location in an area of growing importance to the whole world. The loss was faster on some borders than on some others, but it occurred on all of them. The causes also differed from one border to the next, but all of them stemmed from one single cause, which will be discussed later. But first the evidence of the decline.

To take the two most important parts of the border with India, that is the international border between the Indian and Pakistani sides of Punjab, and the Line of Control in Jammu and Kashmir. On both of them Pakistan's leverage with India increased sharply for some time after Zia's death, because his successors began to move away recklessly from his strategy of lowering the temperature on the Indian border so that Pakistan may more freely pursue his larger aims on the western and north-western side. They adopted the dangerous course of stoking the unrest which had been building up on the Indian side of the borders in Punjab and Kashmir. The initial causes of the unrest lay in the wrong tactics followed by New Delhi in its relations with these two states. But Pakistan saw a welcome opportunity in them for inflicting serious harm upon India at very little cost or risk to itself. Each success that it had, and it did have many up to about the mid-1990s, that is in less than a decade after Zia's death, made Pakistan bolder in this shortsighted adventure.

The inevitable consequence followed. New Delhi woke up to its mistakes, corrected them, dealt with the unrest in both states with greater sensitivity and yet also with more firmness. The unrest in Punjab died down after about seven years of high and dangerous visibility. The trouble in Kashmir persisted for longer, for a time looked more serious because international opinion on it appeared to be more favourable to Pakistan, but the unrest and the foreign support for it declined thereafter. What is more important, India showed Pakistan that one of the military doctrines strongly favoured by the latter was hollow. That further made the

LoC yet another frontier where things went wrong for Pakistan.

This doctrine was that Pakistan could stymie India's superior capability in conventional war with a combination of nuclear threat and unconventional war. Pakistan believed that just as it had been able to find some support among Muslims in the Srinagar valley because India had mishandled the situation there, similarly it could get some support from Muslims elsewhere in India by exploiting its Islamic affinity with them. With their help it could spread the same tentacles of jehadi terrorism in elsewhere in India which had baffled Indian security forces in Kashmir. At the same time, by threatening the use of its nuclear bomb Pakistan could inhibit any attempt by India to use its superiority in conventional arms for launching a punitive attack on Pakistan.

Thus, Pakistan would be left free to exploit Indian Muslims with impunity to spread communal unrest in India as it had done in Kashmir, while it could also use any opportunity it got for using the regular Pakistan army where it was favoured by logistics, the terrain and lack of foresight by India. Pakistan found a combination of all these factors in the mountains of Kargil and launched its army there. But India replied with the full force of its superiority in conventional weapons, including the air force, and Pakistan had to withdraw. In the process Pakistan was also forced to realise that India was prepared to fight a limited war with conventional forces, contrary to the frequently expressed belief among unofficial Indian commentators that there could be no limited war between nuclear weapon countries. This bit of military wisdom for Pakistan was soon followed by a political lesson. In the elections held in Jammu and Kashmir in the autumn of 2002, which the world over were recognised as free and genuine, the vote not only in Jammu but even in Kashmir went strongly in favour of parties which had openly supported the state's continued accession to India.

On the other side, on the Afghan-Pakistan border, the first thing that happened after Zia's death was that Pakistan's own border provinces of NWFP and to a lesser extent Baluchistan became the hinterland of and gave "strategic depth" to the Pushtoon politics of Afghanistan and of these two provinces. Aroused hordes of Pushtoons, most of them trained and equipped under the Taliban movement inspired by Pakistan, moved freely from one country to the other in both directions, and in such large numbers that they reduced the "Durand Line" to a myth. This line had always been held to be a myth by Afghanistan but Pakistan had always considered it to be an inviolable border between NWFP and Afghanistan. The same thing happened to the much longer and much less recognisable border between Afghanistan and Baluchistan, where the Baluchies on the two sides of the border had been groaning under the tyranny of the Pathan.

It is a moot point whether Afghani Pathans took over more of Pakistan or Pakistani Pathans more of Afghanistan. But either way Zia's dream of Afghanistan becoming the "strategic depth" of Pakistan only got an indecent burial somewhere in the wastelands of that region. The Taliban and the regular armed forces of Pakistan did help a lot in driving the Soviet forces out of Afghanistan. But the government which took over the country has even less to do with Pakistan and is less beholden to it than most Afghan governments before it except the Taliban government which ruled over Afghanistan for some time. But even that government, though it began life as the handiwork of Pakistan, soon began to look upon itself as independent and not a proxy of Pakistan. Since then the post-Taliban government of Afghanistan has acquired the opportunity to consolidate its position of total independence from Pakistan. It enjoys widespread international backing, including the backing of all the major powers of the world, which will discourage any country from using it in any manner. It came into being with the support of all the major neighbouring countries, including India in the east, which has regained some of its former position in Afghanistan, Iran in the west, which was a worried neighbour when the Taliban, backed by Pakistan, were running riot in Afghanistan, and the adjoining Central Asian states in the north, which have strong ethnic links with the new government in Kabul.

Among all the neighbours of Afghanistan, Pakistan alone has played a dubious role in the founding of this new Afghanistan, thanks largely to continued commitment of major elements in the Pakistan power structure to the Taliban as well as to its predecessors and successors, such as Gulbuddin Hekmatyar and the Al Qaeda. Hekmatyar was a part of the three horse team through which Pakistan manipulated the Afghan rebellion against Soviet forces. While supporting the rebellion, Pakistan tried to ensure that the successor Afghan authority would be in the hands of Pashtoons, who are close cousins of Pakistan's Pathans, and not in the hands of the northern Tajidks and Uzbeks who have strong links in Central Asia, or the western pro-Iranian tribes based around Herat. Strong evidence of this bias in Pakistan against the Northern Alliance came out during the anti-Soviet rebellion as well as in the formation of the successor government in Kabul. But this manipulation has failed. Instead Afghanistan is now ruled by a government which, recognised and backed by all significant countries, is headed by a Pushtoon leader who is independent of Pakistan. It also has a strong presence of non-Pushtoon leaders who had been earlier opposed by Pakistan. On the other hand Kabul cannot but wonder or worry what to make of reports in influential American newspapers such as the *Washington Post* that Hekmatyar has emerged again in the no-man's land on the Pakistan and Afghanistan border along with "former Taliban and Al Qaeda militants." An American military spokesman has been quoted in the Indian press as telling a Pakistan newspaper, the *Daily Times,* that the Taliban and Hekmatyar are waiting to make a joint push into Afghanistan once America got busy in Iraq.

Therefore there is no chance in the foreseeable future of Pakistan being able to use Afghanistan as a stepping stone to anywhere. And least of all to the Central Asian states. They too, like Afghanistan, would be happy to build such relations with any country, including Pakistan, as their own interests may require. But they would not willingly subordinate themselves to the imperial dreams of any other country. Power equations can influence their relations with only three countries, the United States, Russia, and China, because each of the three is capable of becoming a hegemon in the area. But none of the three would like to promote any other country there except one which can serve the interests of the hegemon, and Pakistan cannot promote the interests of any of the three better than each of the three can do so without depending on Pakistan.

The best example is the United States. Closest to Pakistan at one time, because it depended upon Pakistan for strategic access to Afghanistan and Central Asia, it now has direct and very influential relations with all these countries and a strong military presence of its own wherever it needs one. The same is true of Russia. It had greater control on this area during Soviet days but has better relations with it now. Its relations with Pakistan might improve, and India hopes they will, because Russia's moderating influence on Pakistan would be welcome to India, but Pakistan has no reason for hoping that it will ever replace India in what has been Moscow's vision of South Asia for the past half century. China's vision of South Asia presents an interesting contrast. China used to be described by Pakistan as its most trusted friend. That it still might be, at least in comparative terms. But like Afghanistan, China too has grown wary of its former Pakistan connection because of the suspicion in Beijing that insurrectionist elements in parts of western China are receiving assistance from Islamist radicals in Pakistan. On the other hand not everyone in Pakistan might have forgotten that China did nothing, when it could have done much, to divert India's attention from East Pakistan during the war which led to the emergence of Bangladesh. Or that even on a matter so close to the heart of Pakistan as Kashmir China began to take a position in public in the mid-1990s which did not differ much from India's policy, and Pakistan cannot but have noticed that relations between China and India have improved very noticeably even though China might still see Pakistan as its check upon India.

Pakistan's credentials among the members of the once powerful Organisation of Islamic Countries, OIC, are also not what they used to be. The conservative rulers among them, particularly the unaccountable monarchies, see Al Qaeda type organisations as a threat to their control over their own countries. The radicals among them disapprove of the Pakistan government's support for America's war on Iraq. The progressives dislike what they see as the backward looking conservatism of the Islamist parties in Pakistan, such as the newly risen but potentially powerful MMA, which has formed the governments in the two provinces of Pakistan which adjoin Afghanistan. While America's backing for Pakistan on the one hand and for the conservative Islamic countries on the other used to be something of a bond between the two, now their differing views about the American attack on Iraq have become a cause of disagreement on a very serious issue. Iran has agreed to join India in building a north-south communications corridor just inside Iran from the Iran-Afghan border. Iran's intention is not to by-pass Pakistan but the corridor will greatly nullify a veto Pakistan has been able to impose hitherto on Indian, Iranian, and Afghan efforts to maintain, through Pakistan, the usual economic and political links with each other which are normal between countries which have been made such close neighbours by their geography and history.

What are the causes of this predicament in which Pakistan finds itself, and are there any cures for it ? The real causes are few, but I am afraid the cures are even fewer though that is not to say that there are none at all. The basic cause, which has given birth to many more, is a marriage of inconvenience between an Anglo-American perception, which was mostly right, and a Pakistani perception which was mostly wrong.

There is plenty of literature to show that the idea of Pakistan was born and nurtured in the hot house of a long standing British perception that because of its borders the territory which became West Pakistan would be very useful in the times of tussle with the Soviet Union which would follow soon after the Western Allies and the Soviet Union had defeated their common enemy, Nazi Germany. It was probably a part of the British perception that both parts of divided India would remain a part of the dowry which Britain would bring to this marriage, though as independent countries now and not as parts of the British empire in Asia and Africa. For a time this perception proved right. But not for long.

India would never have taken the path that Pakistan took, of dutifully supporting every Allied move against the Soviet Union and, particularly, against China. But in the earliest stages of its independence India was much more cordial with Britain than with either of the two communist powers, and closer to America than to the Soviet Union. It was only later that the situation changed. When India sought help in building its economic and military potential, it was rebuffed by America and wooed by the Soviet Union. This gave India's strategic options a slant which only became more marked as the contrast between the American and Soviet responses to India's aspirations became sharper. By the mid-1950s the slant hardened into a very durable mould of Indian strategic and foreign policies. This transformation was given a strong push by some distortions in the Anglo-American perceptions on South Asian affairs, including India's role in it and particularly those concerning India, Pakistan, and Kashmir. They also made Anglo-American policies a prisoner of some Pakistani perceptions which were wholly wrong.

America and Britain were committed to one basic assumption : that they could build some anti-Soviet strategies around the CENTO structure, and Pakistan would be a useful eastern abutment for it. If Pakistan demanded Kashmir as the price for its services, Britain and America would go along with that too, for two cold war reasons. First, Kashmir would give them some additional windows into the softer sides of China and the Soviet Union. Second, Pakistan would let them use the windows without asking questions whereas India would like to weigh the pros and cons of every use. But by the mid-1950s it should have become obvious both to Britain and America that they had made a serious misjudgment in weighing India and Pakistan in the cold war scales.

If they had carefully weighed how useful Pakistan had really been to them for their military strategies in the actual conditions in the 1950s, as against the uses envisaged in some outdated British strategic thinking in the inter-war years, and if they had also factored in their cold war politics in the developing world, they might have made a better judgement. It was only a quarter century later, when the Soviet Union made the mistake of marching its troops into Afghanistan, that the western tilt in favour Pakistan paid some dividends. But even that advantage was blown when America made its customary blunderbuss approach to Afghan politics and Pakistan messed it up further by its support for the blunderbuss itself, namely the Taliban. The world, including America, is still paying the price of these mistakes. Fortunately for India and America, the lesson of these mistakes was not lost upon America, as proved by the changes in its relations with and assessments of India in the 1990s. America's perceptions might have been clouded again in the last couple of years by the unbalanced approach by America to the Pakistan connection with terrorism. The current American President thinks Pakistan is part of the solution to the problem, whereas in reality it is part of the problem itself, a point which merits elaboration a little later. But it will not be long before that cloud also goes the way or the earlier ones, as it was doing before the terrorist attack on the World Trade Centre in New York.

As for Pakistani perceptions in the early 1950s, which were wholly wrong as stated earlier, they have proved to be not only wholly wrong but also tragic, for India, for Kashmir, and most of all for Pakistan itself. Contrary to the way Pakistan saw it, under the British scheme, according to which India was divided with no reference to the religion of the people concerned, the inhabitants of certain designated territories of what was known as "British India" were given the option to decide whether to join India or Pakistan. As for "Indian India", that it is the princely states, also called "Indian states", each ruler was left free to decide, again without reference to the religion of his subjects, whether he wanted his state to accede to India or to Pakistan (the option to remain independent was also mentioned in passing). Each rulers was advised however to opt for the country to which his state was contiguous.

The state of Jammu and Kashmir was contiguous to both India and to what was to become Pakistan. The ruler opted for India. Pakistan insisted he should have opted for Pakistan because, it argued, the Muslims were in majority in the state (which they are, though by a small margin). This misperception on the part of Pakistan would have been short lived and harmless if Pakistan had not launched attacks on the state, in 1947-48, first by tribals, then by tribals plus irregulars and finally by the regular Pakistan army in an effort to prevent the ruler from acceding to India. Even that might not have mattered too much for too long because the attack would have been thrown back, as indeed it was. But Pakistan continued the attacks, whether they came in the form of regular attacks by the Pakistan army, as in 1965, or genocidal, plus demographic plus military, as in 1971. Each attack was defeated, but each added further bitterness in the relations between the two countries. International politics added their own complications. Encouraged in this by the anti-Soviet games of the United States, Pakistan continued to disobey the resolutions of the United Nations on Kashmir though they had been accepted by India. Ten years of this game drove the United Nations itself to the conclusion, in 1957, that the resolutions had become inoperable.

It is arguable that President Zia's strategy in the mid-1980s might have deflected Pakistan's energies to his vision of an Islamic empire in Central Asia. But one part of that strategy proved more poisonous for the relations between India and Pakistan, and for the problem of Kashmir, than perhaps he intended. He tried to build up domestic support for his strategy by harnessing it to his programme of Islamisation at home through his concept of "Nizam-e-Mustapha" for Pakistan. This had three very damaging consequences, most of all damaging for Pakistan but also for Kashmir and for the rest of India in varying degrees. The concept gave an increasingly marked Islamic twist to the domestic polity of Pakistan, and the supporters as well as opponents of Zia, for their own varying reasons, adopted it as their principal activity. The supporters thought they would thereby reinforce his Central Asian vision, the opponents hoped they would weaken him by disabling his effort to disengage from India and Kashmir in order to turn his attention westwards.

The effect in India was that the sounds of Islamic fury coming from across the border stirred communal angers in India. In Kashmir it was that the secular aim of "azadi" got a jehadi colour, and the Government of India found it increasingly difficult to work a compromise acceptable in New Delhi, Srinagar, and Jammu. In Pakistan the rift between the governments of the day and vociferously Islamic elements became wider and wider, and Islamabad became increasingly disinclined and certainly unable to control those very bands of militants which it had been training and arming for activities across Pakistan's borders with Afghanistan and India. This means that Pakistan lost all three of the qualifications it needed, as mentioned at the start of this paper, for using its strategically located borders for its maximum advantage. Stronger than India it never was and cannot become. Its control over its borders became weaker and weaker. All hope of improvement in relations with neighbours went into a tailspin as each jehadi attack received the expected response from India and in Afghanistan it triggered a chain of events which Zia might never have dreamt of.

Everyone is well aware of what has been happening to Pakistan's domestic politics for the past two decades or so. But an updated assessment has now come from a highly qualified source which no one can accuse of being anti-Pakistan or pro-India or pro-Afghanistan : the International Crisis Group, based in Brussels. The Group issued a long report, dated March 20, 2003, on the situation in Pakistan, and also at the same time released a brief summary of its own for the media, entitled "The Mullahs and the Military". In it the Group says "The International Crisis Group warns that an alliance of major religious parties threatens to undermine civil liberties, freedom of expression, legal reforms and religious tolerance in Pakistan. The situation of women and minorities is of particular concern."

"The Mujtahida Majlis-e-Amal (MMA) was elected to government in the North-West Frontier Province (NWFP) and Baluchistan in October 2002. Its leaders vow to Islamise state and society, counter to President Musharraf's pledges to end religious extremism. However, MMA's zeal is not being confronted by the President or the military, while the President's recent constitutional amendments have undermined the domestic standing of moderate secular parties – to the benefit of the religious lobby."

"While moderate sections of Pakistani society are being marginalised, religious parties and their causes are flourishing. The religious right, jihad and Islamisation are acceptable currencies in political life. ICG urges donors to channel their funding through the federal government to women and minorities in NWFP and Baluchistan and to link funding to the state of fundamental freedoms in MMA governments."

"The dangers of inaction are evident. The MMA leaders have deferred to the military in setting foreign and security policy but may in the end be unable to curb the anti-American sentiments of their followers. Pakistan could then find itself isolated regionally and a target, as opposed to a partner, in the US-led war against terrorism."

In the course of the summary, ICG's South Asia Project Director, Samina Ahmad, is quoted as saying : "Since the military take over in 1999, the government has demonstrated neither the will nor intent to pursue domestic policies opposed by the mullahs, such as madrasa regulation or changes in discriminatory Islamic laws. The perpetual threat of war with India over Kashmir also brings the mullahs and the military close together."

The ICG Asia Programme Director, Robert Templer, is quoted as saying, "The federal government will have to restrain MMA provincial governments from inciting jihadi sentiments and encouraging a gun culture in the name of local traditions. More pressure from key donors might expedite the disarmament of jihadi groups and ending their activities." Internal opinion in Pakistan shares the foreboding of the ICG, as can be seen in two articles by the present author which are based on extracts from the Pakistan press. The extracts also show how deep is the realisation in Pakistan now that the country has lost much of the leverage it had acquired in earlier years from its strategic location in an important region of the world.

But why has Pakistan, which began with a reasonably good potential for viability and progress, committed itself to this suicidal course ? It is difficult to find a clear answer to that question in politics but perhaps an analogy from psychiatry might help. Starting with a misperception of the reasons why the state of Jammu and Kashmir acceded to India, and reaching an equally rigid misperception of its ability to capture the state by a military hook or a political crook, Pakistan became the victim of a problem which is well known to students of child psychology, that a disorientation sets in in a person if he has a constant ambition which constantly exceeds his grasp. No reasoning helps then nor the direct evidence of repeated experiences. But the case is not as hopeless as the analogy might suggest, because of late some realistic counsels have been appearing in the Pakistan press, as shown in the attached articles. Neither the diagnosis appearing in the press nor the remedies prescribed by the authors of these comments have provoked a rejectionist approach by the people of Pakistan, which means there is room for recovery yet.

There have also been a few signs of late that a greater sense of realism is growing where it matters most, that is not only within the military but within that wing of the military, the key intelligence coordinator, the Inter-Services Intelligence (ISI), which for years has been suspected to be in charge of the jehadi off shoots of the Pakistan civil and military establishment. This possibility (it cannot be described as much more than a possibility yet) has grown further in the context of the successful elections in Jammu and Kashmir last year. But signs of it had appeared a little earlier also and have been discussed at greater length in the present author's extended paper for the Centre for Policy Research, New Delhi, entitled "Kashmir in Changing Perspectives". But the immediately relevant portions of it are reproduced below.

"An interesting ripple took place in the politics of Pakistan about the time that reports began to appear that the people of Kashmir were responding with enthusiasm to the prospect of a credible election in the state. As in the case of the example given earlier regarding the impact of the elections in Kashmir on PoK, there is no clear evidence here either for relating the elections in Kashmir directly to this development in the politics of Pakistan. Yet there might be something more than a mere coincidence here also. At the time of the early reports on the probable reaction of the people of Kashmir to the prospects of election, an important Pakistani soldier, General Assad Durrani, former chief of the all-important military establishment in Pakistan, ISI, sent a significant paper to a mainly Indo-Pakistan conference on South Asian Security which was held in Geneva at the beginning of November, 2002, that is within days of the publication of the results of the election which confirmed the earlier reports of keenness among Kashmiri voters to participate. In addition to his generally constructive approach to Indo-Pakistan Security issues, General Durrani departed noticeably in his paper from the policy line laid down by General Mussharraf regarding the outcome of the Lahore summit between Mr Vajpayee and Mr. Nawaz Sharrif, Prime Ministers of India and Pakistan, and in particular toward the Lahore Declaration and the MoU signed between the two countries.

These are the two most helpful documents signed between the two countries on security issues, and the only ones which also make an attempt to address the nuclear equation between them. Immediately after the summit meeting, General Musharraf deposed Prime Minister Nawaz Sharrif and made himself yet another military dictator of his country. That however should have made no difference to the validity of Pakistan's signatures on the two documents. But General Musharraf sweepingly denounced both and added them to the heap of broken agreements between the two countries. Against that background it was refreshing to hear General Durrani describe them as an 'opportunity (which) was squandered' and a chance for 'overall progress' which was lost. Refreshing enough for me to suggest that in the light of his opinion about the two documents perhaps he should be invited by the conference to confer with some Indian counterparts to see if the opportunity could be resuscitated. That the suggestion did not lead to the anything is only a small part of the unfortunate story of India and Pakistan."

(Extract ends)

2

Changing Perspectives on Kashmir

The Impact of Three Recent Elections

Events in Jammu and Kashmir, and the processes which shape them, are a difficult subject to comment on. Perspectives change continuously, and in recent times have changed faster than earlier. They are also moulded by factors, domestic and foreign, which are rarely transparent, while opinions about them are so strong at times that they further cloud the vision. At the same time few subjects are more important than this for India to comprehend as clearly as may be possible.

Few events affect India's internal and external relations as much or as fast as those in and about the state of Jammu and Kashmir and the reactions to them, whether among Indians or among India's friends and foes, whether near or far. Assessments have to be updated without waiting for potent but fleeting events to get the stamp of proof from history. Room has to be left for conjecture and speculation, while also ensuring that conclusions are drawn objectively.

It is for these reasons that in the following pages few attempts have been made to re-visit the distant past as scholars of history may do. The focus has been kept on a few, selected, and recent events which, though the progeny of a distant past, are more important in terms of their influence on the foreseeable future. Few policy prescriptions have been attempted, though such lessons which have been left us by past mistakes and successes have been flagged.

In the end, a word of apology. These pages have been written by someone who is addicted to commenting more quickly on current events. Therefore much that is contained in them has been published before. But instead of dressing it up in new words, it has been allowed to stand in without change of clothes. That makes the plagiarism more blatant. But it is plagiarism from my own writing.

The issue of the future of the state of Jammu and Kashmir raises a number of other issues, including the diplomatic, strategic, and security concerns of many countries in addition to the two most directly concerned, that is India and Pakistan. The perspectives in which they may be seen extend many decades into the past and probably as deeply into the future as well. To discuss all of them in their fullness would be a huge undertaking.

I have therefore tried to place them in the limited perspective of some recent developments. These, however, are very potent developments and for many separate reasons. One, they are among the developments which have powerfully affected the future of Jammu and Kashmir, and particularly of Kashmir, more than any other in the recent past have done. Second, they have altered, and have been altered by, the most dynamic element in the current situation, namely the preferences of the people concerned. Third, thoughts about them are supported by some concrete evidence.

Even out of these, I have chosen mainly three developments because, more clearly than many others, all three qualify by the three criteria I have mentioned here. These developments are, or relate to, three elections held in very recent months, the ones in Kashmir, in Pakistan, and most recently in Gujarat. The first two elections have a major bearing on the relations between New Delhi and Srinagar, and on the relations between India and Pakistan, which are the background against which the Kashmir issue is played out. The third is also related, though less directly. The three elections together are more important as formative events than the three main Indo-Pakistan events involving violence and military action in recent months, that is the Kargil war, the attack on the Indian Parliament, and the mobilisation by the two countries which followed. I will first describe the main features of each election, then its impact these Kashmir perspectives, and then try some fragmentary thoughts on how they might affect future relations between the three corners of the Little Triangle, New Delhi, Srinagar, and Islamabad, including any war-like thoughts that might arise anywhere within or around the triangle.

First, the *Elections in Pakistan*, and their impact, respectively, on Pakistan, on India as a whole, and on the Jammu and Kashmir part of it.

The Impact on Pakistan

These elections were held in some very unfavourable circumstances. By the time they were held, the President and Chief of the Army Staff of Pakistan, General Musharraf, had taken all democratic teeth out of the Constitution and insured himself against the consequences of any adverse verdict, a fact denounced by many foreign observers, including those sent by the European Union. Also, they were held when he had further insured himself against even the possibility of such a verdict by crippling the electoral capabilities of the two most important opposition leaders in Pakistan, former Prime Ministers Mrs Benazir Bhutto and Mr Nawaz Sharif, who alone had been Prime Ministers for more than one term.

The participation of these two important national leaders in politics was severely restricted by General Musharraf, when, as chief of the Pakistan Army, he deposed the Prime Minister of the day, Mr Nawaz Sharif, and put the country back under full military rule. A short time before the election on October 10, General Musharraf also imposed similar restrictions on the Pakistan People's Party, the party of Mrs Benazir Bhutto, and the Muslim League, the party of Mr Nawaz Sharif, which are the two main opposition parties. Left standing in the name of each party was a splinter of each which he had first rendered harmless.

These events, coupled with the low turn out of voters, ended the credibility of the elections even before they were held, and the outcome, a forgone conclusion as it was, received a very poor rating at home and abroad. Official America, mainly concerned with the support it expected from Pakistan in fighting the Taliban stragglers along the Afghan-Pakistan border, praised General Musharraf, for holding the elections at all instead of taking a closer look at the kind of elections these were. But the more knowledgeable and impartial in all countries realised that the opposition space left after the two main opposition parties and their leaders had been sidelined by the General was left free to be occupied, and came to be occupied in the elections, by some ultra conservative and religion based groupings which were hardly distinguishable from the Taliban in their political personality.

There have always been violent and fanatical supporters or opponents of various sectarian factions of Islam in Pakistan, whether they are seen as true Islamists or not. They have often been close to what has come to be known as the politics of jehad, and as such their rise to positions of political power has always had some dangerous implications for India and more particularly for Jammu and Kashmir. In most earlier elections they had been noticed mainly as noisy agitators, more able to motivate crowds than voters. But in this election their joint front, MMA, emerged as the third largest element in the National Assembly, as the majority party in NWFP, and as the biggest party by far in Baluchistan.

These two of the four provinces of Pakistan border Afghanistan, have been the cradle of the Taliban movement, and next only to Afghanistan have been of the greatest concern to the international alliance against terrorism. Some off-shoots of these forces in the extreme east of Pakistan have been of concern to China, just as those in north-western Pakistan and in northern Afghanistan have worried Russia and its neighbours in Central Asia. Therefore capture of important seats of political power by them in Pakistan was rightly seen in India as a danger signal for India in general and for Jammu and Kashmir in particular.

Instead of bringing much credit to Pakistan for restoring democracy, these latest elections evoked scepticism because of the remarkably low turn out of voters, estimated to be only about 10 per cent or only about half of even the previous low in which Mr Nawaz Sharif was able to contrive a huge mandate in the National Assembly. That apart, the elections have redoubled the process which has been going on in Pakistan for a long time by which the domestic politics of Pakistan have been getting radicalised in favour of religious extremism. The process began in a milder form many years ago when Pakistan, failing to dislodge India from Kashmir militarily, in the wars of 1947-48 and 1965, stepped up Islamic fervour in South Asian politics as its roadway into Kashmir. The more it did so the more Pakistan's international and domestic politics acquired an Islamic slant, and the more that happened the more Indian politics responded with an opposite slant. The result was to be seen quite soon in the last of the three elections under discussion here, namely the one in Gujarat.

Pakistan's basic premise was, and remains, that since Muslims are in majority in the state of Jammu and Kashmir, and particularly in the province of Kashmir, the state as a whole or at least the province of Kashmir should be given to Pakistan. This demand has been the fulcrum of Pakistan's domestic politics, the engine which has driven Pakistan's wars against India, and has been used by all of Pakistan's parties ever since the county was created, and by the Islamist parties in more recent decades to Talibanise the polity of Pakistan. This process is now a familiar part of South Asian history but needs some recapitulation as the background to even more recent developments, such as Pakistan's demand for mediation in Kashmir and India's refusal of the same.

Pakistan's argument that it should get Kashmir because it has a Muslim majority ignores the whole scheme by which the provinces of British India were divided between India and Pakistan in 1947, and the princely states were given the right to decide whether to accede to India or Pakistan, or even to remain independent if they chose to do so. The partition scheme devised by the British Parliament and accepted by all the major parties of India and by all parties in what was to become Pakistan made no reference at all to the religions of the people of undivided India or of the princely states.

The partition scheme only delineated certain territories of British India and left it to the elected legislatures of these territories to decide whether to form a part of Pakistan or India, and a referendum was to be held in those territories which did not have elected legislatures at that time. That is why even the people of the North-West Frontier Province of Pakistan, in which Muslims were in an overwhelming majority, did not automatically get the right to join Pakistan. They had to decide to do so by referendum.

In the case of the princely states also, no reference was made to the religion of the people. It was left to the ruler of the state to decide whether the state should join India or Pakistan or become independent, though informally they were advised to join the country, India or Pakistan, with which they were contiguous and not to opt for independence because that would be an unsustainable choice. The ruler of Jammu and Kashmir also got the same right. He was assured by the

Government of India that it would have be no objection if he opted for Pakistan, was also given time beyond the deadline laid down by the British Parliament for a decision, but was also advised not to delay his decision for too long.

He delayed it till nearly the end of the eleventh hour, and might have asked, and received, more time, if Pakistan had not tried to hustle him by launching an attack on Kashmir through hordes of tribal raiders from NWFP, supported by regulars of the Pakistan army. Fearing for his own safety and his independence to decide, he asked for military help from India but was rightly told that Indian soldiers could not be sent for the defence of a foreign territory and against a neighbour with which India was not at war. It was only then, with the raiders at the gates of the state capital, Srinagar, within gun range of the airfield, which was the only possible link Srinagar still had with India, however tenuously, that he acceded to India. It was only in the nick of time that Indian soldiers got there to defend it in what remains probably the most daring airlift in South Asia.

Having missed that bus Pakistan demanded a plebiscite in Kashmir at the United Nations. There was no such provision either in the British Parliament's Act or in international practice. But with Pakistan a military ally now of the United States and India seen to be on the side of the Soviet Union in the cold war configuration of the Security Council, the United Nations decreed in favour of a UN supervised plebiscite. India accepted the unjust and unwarranted decree, but on the basis of conditions which are clearly reflected in the scheme of the decree and were reinforced by written assurances to India. However, the prospect of a plebiscite set up such a wave of Islamic rhetoric in Pakistan that it submerged the country's domestic politics for decades to come. This communal slant in Pakistan only became more and more pronounced with the passage of time.

On this basis Pakistan claimed victory when the UN

resolutions of the late 1940s were passed. Unfortunately the simplicity of this propaganda plus its own strategic interests in the Cold War, which had already begun, misled the United States and its Allies into believing that perhaps it would be useful for them if the strategic area of Kashmir, so close to the underbelly of the Soviet Union and on a strategic flank of the oil rich countries of the Middle East, went to such a staunch ally in the Cold War as Pakistan had become. How perfidious was the role this consideration in the British manoeuvures for the partition of India has been brought out in the well researched book, *War and Diplomacy in Kashmir*, by C. Dasgupta (Sage, India, 2002)

So strong was the *real politique* of this self-interest that it persuaded the Allies to ignore one basic fact about these resolutions : that India accepted them, and Pakistan killed them while pretending to accept them. The resolutions laid down three essential conditions which Pakistan must fulfill before India could be asked to hold a plebiscite. That is, it must withdraw its armed forces from the whole of Jammu and Kashmir, must assist in bringing about withdrawal of the irregulars who entered the state through Pakistan (and with the assistance of Pakistan as India contended) and must let the J&K Government which had acceded to India extend its administration over the whole state. The UN also assured India separately that it would not be obliged to hold a plebiscite until Pakistan fulfilled these conditions India would not be obliged to hold a plebiscite in the state. Pakistan violated each of the three conditions then, continued to violate them – and continues right up to this day — until the UN itself was driven to the conclusion that the resolutions could no longer be carried out, as recorded by a mediator appointed by the United Nations.

But in the meantime the domestic politics of Pakistan had been cast into such a hard mould of religion that it became the fulcrum of the country's domestic as well as

South Asian politics. As if that were not bad enough, the two wars that have swept through Afghanistan, one by and the other against the Taliban version of Islam, locked the whole of the north-west of South Asia into a wider arc of the same mould, subjecting the India-Pakistan relations to further tensions. Now the latest elections in Pakistan have done more of the same because of the success of the extreme right wing parties, which has been described above. They have become an important element in the government of Pakistan and, even more, in the governments of the two provinces of Pakistan which matter more in this context because they are contiguous to Afghanistan and are a part of the whole area which lies astride the border between the two countries and is believed to be the haven of the remnants of the Taliban.

It is difficult to tell how these parties will behave. Parties often behave differently when aspiring to be in the harness of office than when fated only to be in the opposition. Even so, their leaders have lost no time in lifting the veil on their intentions. The national leader of MMA, the alliance of Islamist parties, Fazlur Rehman, was asked at a press meet early in November, 2002, whether the Alliance would want America to withdraw its troops from Pakistan. He said the stand of the Alliance was spelt out in the manifesto, and the question whether American troops would withdraw should now be addressed to America. The Alliance Chief Minister in the Frontier Province, the most relevant of the four provinces of Pakistan in this context, said at another meet he would ask America 'to respect the opinion of the people of the province and stop operations against Al Qaeda and Taliban suspects." (*The Hindu*, 4.11.002) All this should worry both Islamabad and Kabul. And Washington no less, where experts on South Asia must wonder how President Musharraf will juggle with issues of survival while trying to keep the MMA in good humour and at the same time be an effective partner of President Bush in the campaign against the Al Qaeda, which Bush wishes to root out in NWFP among other places.

President Bush could, of course, tempt Musharraf to remain by his side by making him a more visible partner in the unfolding American design for refashioning the whole oil rich part of the Muslim world, extending right up into Central Asia. This was also the unrealised dream of General-President Zia, who seems to be a role model for Musharraf. But that should worry Islamabad and Washington more than New Delhi and Srinagar. Pakistan needs to worry as it ponders over the options left for it in the wake of the mess left behind by its own creation, the Taliban. Such carrots as it might get as America's partner in the post 9.11 world would hardly compensate it for the corrosion of its polity which its increased Talibanisation will cause. This danger will only increase if preoccupation with Iraq draws America away from the Afghan-Pakistan border and the Taliban phenomenon takes root there again. Hence the anxiety reflected in the statement by the British Foreign Minister that India should leave Pakistan free to deal with the existing Taliban phenomenon. But the root of the problem does not lie in what India may do or be dissuaded from doing. It lies in the soil of Pakistan, and in the tension which has developed in operational relations between American and Pakistani forces as they jointly hunt for Al Qaeda stragglers in the no-man's land along the Afghan-Pakistan border. America and Pakistan have papered over some of these clashes in the agreement they announced on 6.01.03 on hot pursuit into Pakistan by American forces. But this is a fire which can be re-lighted by the rising influence of the radical Islamist parties of Pakistan in this very border area, particularly if a war flares up over Iraq.

Another interesting development also took place in the politics of Pakistan about the time that reports began to appear that the people of Kashmir were responding with enthusiasm to the prospect of credible elections in the state. There is no direct evidence for relating this development to the elections. But the coincidence of the events might not be entirely accidental. At the time that the people of the state were showing keen interest in the elections, an important

Pakistani soldier, General Assad Durrani, former chief of the all-important military establishment in Pakistan, ISI, sent a significant paper to a mainly Indo-Pakistan conference on South Asian Security which was held in Geneva at the beginning of November, 2002, that is within days of the publication of the results of the elections. In addition to his generally constructive approach to Indo-Pakistan security issues, General Durrani departed noticeably in his paper from the policy line laid down by General Musharraf regarding the outcome of the Lahore summit between Mr Vajpayee and Mr. Nawaz Sharrif, Prime Ministers of India and Pakistan, and in particular regarding the Lahore Declaration and the MoU signed between the two countries.

These are the two most helpful documents signed between the two countries on security issues, and the only ones which also make an attempt to address the nuclear equation between them. Immediately after the summit meeting, General Musharraf deposed Prime Minister Nawaz Sharrif and made himself yet another military dictator of his country. That however should have made no difference to the validity of Pakistan's signatures on the two documents. But General Musharraf sweepingly denounced both and added them to the heap of broken agreements between the two countries. Against that background it was refreshing to hear General Durrani describe them as an "opportunity (which) was squandered" and a chance for "overall progress" which was lost. Refreshing enough for me to suggest — at the conference — that in the light of his opinion about the two documents, perhaps he should be invited by the conference to confer with some Indian counterparts to see if the opportunity could be resuscitated. That my suggestion was not taken up is only a minor one among the opportunities which have been squandered in South Asia. But soon after the elections an interesting development also occurred on the Pakistan side of Kashmir which will be discussed later in this paper.

The Impact on India

What India has to watch more closely now is whether

President Musharraf will yield to the temptation of easing MMA's pressure upon him by letting, or even encouraging MMA to divert its energies to Kashmir. This had been the traditional destination of fanatical raiders from Pakistan, going all the way back to the days of the partition of India. But it was tested out more recently also when the collapse of the Taliban regime in Afghanistan persuaded Pakistan to create some occupation on the Indian side for the Taliban who were retreating into Pakistan, particularly for those of the Taliban who were of Pakistani origin, among whom were many Pakistani soldiers disguised as Taliban. It was noticeable for instance that as the rout of the militants in Afghanistan gathered pace, there was an increase in the number of those who were being pushed into Kashmir.

Hence the concern in India over reports in the wake of the collapse of the Taliban in Afghanistan that a few hundred Taliban, who were probably of Pakistani origin, had been secretly airlifted to Pakistan under the cover of darkness from a fort in northern Afghanistan which had been surrounded by the forces of the Northern Alliance. The obviously worrisome aspect for India was that these battle hardened Taliban would be headed for Kashmir sooner rather than later. But what made the reports more worrying was the as yet unanswered question whether their escape had been connived at by the American and other western forces in Afghanistan. These forces had already established complete air control over Afghanistan and no rescue plane could have lifted anyone away without the American eyes looking the other way.

Further suspicions have appeared since those events : increasing activity by radicalised Islamists and Pakistani and other Taliban in this area, the recurring clashes between them and American soldiers, leading to strong anti-American demonstrations in Pakistan, and pressing requests by America to India not to press Pakistan too hard on this issue despite India's anxiety about what their activity means for security and peace in Kashmir. They are most active in those very areas of Pakistan which, as mentioned earlier, adjoin Afghanistan and where they have gained influence in the local governments. Pakistan's options in this situation are either to join hands with India in ending the Kashmir dispute, or to keep up the pressure of terrorism on Kashmir and India. The latter choice would obviously damage Pakistan's polity still further, and put its survival at risk if continued terrorism against India triggered another war with India, or if a still more hardened brand of the Taliban swallowed the polity of Pakistan.

The Impact on Jammu and Kashmir

The impact on the state has generally been the same as on India as a whole, namely the danger that the Islamist parties, using such infiltration as they can manage among Indian Muslims, may generate more communal discord in India than they have managed to do already. Or, given their hold on the more turbulent population of NWFP and Baluchistan, may add their own religious zeal to the military objectives with which General Musharraf started the Kargil war, and therefore terrorism might be practiced against India with greater intensity. Relations between the two countries will then freeze further. But there are two specific aspects which concern the state more particularly, and both have been further complicated by the increased presence of extremist elements in the polity of Pakistan.

First, there is much less chance than there ever was that the Kashmiri separatist groups gathered under the umbrella of the Hurriyat will ever be able to bridge the gap between India and Pakistan. There will be less room for them in the councils of Pakistan, and less willingness in India to see any scope for a helpful role by them. Second, there will be a further setback for the proposition favoured by some third parties that the problem be solved by dividing the state between India and Pakistan more or less along the Line of Control. The proposition has never been very popular in India even politically. But even less so is it in terms of its practicality, or rather the lack of it, because it proposes what is logistically absurd, that the LoC should become a more open or at least a more porous border between the two portions of the state while the international border between the two countries may remain as hard as it is. Since each portion of the state has an open border with the country in which it is located, allowing the people of India or Pakistan to move freely into their side of the state, any openings in the LoC would become openings between the two countries. This means that a porous LoC and a tight international border cannot co-exist. They must be relaxed or hardened in tandem.

Next, the *elections in Jammu and Kashmir*, and their impact on the state, on the rest of India, and on Pakistan.

The Impact on Kashmir

The elections in Jammu and Kashmir were unprecedented in some ways and most unusual in some. They were unprecedented because for the first time in the state the ballot box clearly gave a negative verdict on the government, and the government quit. This had happened innumerable times in other states of the Indian Union, and in the past quarter century has been happening at the national level also, more often than not. But in Jammu and Kashmir it happened for the very first time in October last year.

In the earliest elections in the state the government of Sheikh Mohammad Abdullah had been truly popular and for this reason invincible, and though his popularity might have declined in later years he bounced back in the mid-1970s when a genuine political process began once again under a good political settlement between him and Prime Minister Indira Gandhi. The mantle of this settlement was creditably carried by his son and successor, Farooq Abdullah, and hopes of a better turn in the relations between Srinagar and New Delhi conferred such popularity upon him that he won some good elections even when Mrs Gandhi herself actively campaigned against him in the state, as in 1983. In later years however he invited trouble by subverting elections to perpetuate his rule, raised a storm of protest from the people of the state, allowed the administration to be ruined by corruption, inefficiency and insensitivity, and the wheel of democracy finally turned against him in the elections in the state last October.

But it is not merely that one government fell and another came in, or that both did so through the ballot box, or that in the process the only separatist organisation in Kashmir, the Hurriyat, was unable to hide that it stood totally isolated from the mainstream of politics in the valley. But the issues changed, and so did the nature of the elections. So also did the fortunes of war. New Delhi had turned a blind eye on his doings in Kashmir so long as India faced a credible security threat from Pakistan through Kashmir, either a direct threat on the battlefield, as in the attack Pakistan mounted surreptitiously in the mountains of Kargil, or an indirect threat by stoking an armed insurgency against India. But Pakistan gradually lost out on both fronts, and as a result New Delhi decided that it was no longer necessary to go along with the games Farooq had been playing with elections.

Similarly that part of the militancy which was more rooted in Kashmir also began to shake off the reins which were held in Pakistan. Militarily, Pakistan was fought out of Kargil. Soon afterwards Pakistan also found itself on the wrong side of the dividing line in the politics of the militancy in Kashmir. This was shown when, beginning about two years ago, the cadres of militancy based in Kashmir, responding to the trends of change in the public opinion in Kashmir itself, began to distance themselves from the leaders of the cadres based in and controlled by Pakistan, and it happened again towards the end of 2002, near the time of the Muslim festival of Id. On both occasions the Kashmiri militants based in the valley defied the instructions of the jehadi council based in Pakistan and declared a cease-fire either on their own or in response to similar gestures by the Indian security forces.

Then came the latest election, which made it clear that the majority of the people of Kashmir are not looking forward to being conquered either directly by the Pakistan army or indirectly through bands of fanatical jehadis, whose idea of Islam is very different from the gentler version which had flourished for centuries in Kashmir. Most Kashmiris are united behind a desire for a peaceful life of political rights and economic development after the resolution of an unending dispute. They are divided only on the best way to get there and only in that sense have an interest in Indo-Pakistan problems. A small but vociferous minority does support Pakistan for what it is, and drives others by the fear of its guns. But it has been checkmated by the spectacle of Pakistan's defeat in battle, the success of the Indian security forces against the militants and terrorists, and now the verdict of the ballot box.

Some statements a few months ago, by General Padmanabhan, at that time Chief of Staff of the Indian army, that there had been a sharp decline in the attacks in and on Kashmir by Pakistan based militants and terrorists were probably premature, as shown by the casualties that are still being inflicted on Indian security forces through exploding devices and on the civilian population by land-mines and in surprise raids in remote areas. But the outcome of the election in Jammu and Kashmir has certainly deprived these attacks of the veil of legitimacy Pakistan was able to put upon them as long as it could claim that the people of Kashmir were opposed to India.

The outcome of the election is both a proof and a consequence of these slowly maturing changes in public opinion in Kashmir. The outcome was blunted to some extent by the explosive power displayed by the militants on the eve and the morning of election and at the doorstep of polling zones, particularly in some urban areas of high population density. They succeeded in scaring away a higher turn out in many areas, although there were urban pockets of core support for the militants in which voters stayed away out of conviction. But even so the overall turn out in Kashmir reached 44 per cent which, considering the circumstances, is reasonably high, compared with the turn out in the state as a whole, which was a couple points higher, and in the Hindu majority province of Jammu, which was still higher by a few points.

This may surprise those who have convinced themselves that the only question in Kashmir is whether the state should remain a part of India or leave it to join Pakistan (or at least to become independent). But even supporters of the Pakistan or the independence option never raised it up front as an election issue, and it did not figure in the platform of any participating party. There was nothing in the electoral rules which could have prevented them from raising it, and no one complained that he was prevented from raising it. However, the issue began to emerge, and then it did so significantly, as the campaigns got under way. And as it did it gave an added significance to the statistics of the outcome.

Most of those who boycotted the election by intention, or tried to intimidate others into boycotting it, were groups and parties known to be against any election under the Indian Constitution. All those who voted or campaigned in favour of doing so were either declared supporters of the Indian connection or were declaring they were more interested in good governance than in the colour of the government. Therefore, if you take away the usual abstentions from any election for non-political reasons, the percentage of those who made an anti-India statement by abstaining is significantly lower than the percentage of those who made an opposite statement by casting their votes, and decided to do so knowing full well the physical dangers they would face in doing it. Sure, they did so out of mixed motives, and many were voting against Farooq Abdullah, not for India; for better governance and not for continued accession to India. But generally those who voted at all were not voting against India. This point was underscored by the defeat of all of the few known militants who did decide to enter the electoral contest in the guise of "independents."

Only a few months earlier an international opinion poll, the first in Jammu and Kashmir and carried out by "Facts Worldwide, an affiliate of MORI in India", had given the estimate, as reported in *The Hindu* newspaper of June 1, 2002, that 86 per cent of the people polled wanted that militancy and the infiltration from across the border should end, and 61 per cent wanted to remain Indian citizens. At that time the estimate seemed hard to believe, but not after the election results came out. For these reasons it is even more significant than it might have been otherwise, that a large majority of the vote in the whole of the state, and a clear majority even in Kashmir was polled by the National Conference, the Congress, and some other parties whose support for the state's accession to India is unambiguous and unconditional, and by independents who had jumped in as individuals only because they had been denied the ticket by these parties. Another large chunk was polled by a significant new party, the People's Democratic Party, whose top priority is not secession but open door and open ended talks with all who are committed to a peaceful resolution of the "problem", and no political party, whether based in the state or anywhere else in the country is opposed to the essentials of the PDP position.

With this election the people of Kashmir have been given a clear proof that they can elect a government of their choice if they decide to exercise their democratic right to vote without being deterred by the threats of militants. This restoration of the democratic process in the state is a more important outcome of the election than the change of government.. However, for the continued faith of the people in the process, it is also important that now there is a government in the state which has all of these seven credits : first, it has been elected by clearly democratic means ; second, consists of parties which do not question the state's accession to India ; third, is a coalition between one party which is strong in the valley and another which is strong in Jammu, since these are the two most important regions of the state; fourth, has a Chief Minister who is from the valley and a Deputy Chief Minister who is from Jammu ; fifth, is also backed by a majority of the people of the valley if you add up the votes polled in the valley by the PDP, the Congress and by those independents who belonged to these two parties till their failure to get the party ticket; sixth, for the first time since the early 1950s, among those who voted an even bigger majority in the valley than in the state as a whole voted for parties and independents who did not oppose the state's accession to India; and seventh, for the first time ever a major Indian national party, the Congress, is a partner in a democratically elected government in the state.

Of course, it is possible that some of these advantages will be diluted or even nullified by any of several possible developments. The two which are the most difficult to rule out are friction between the coalition partners in Srinagar, and between Srinagar and New Delhi. Each of these dangers can become sharper if the Pakistan sponsored insurgency assumes such a shape or form that the Congress within Kashmir or the Union government in New Delhi finds such counter-measures to be necessary as the PDP considers difficult to live with. Or if PDP embraces such a vision of Kashmir's place in the Indian Union which either the Union government or the Congress cannot live with. There is also the danger that Srinagar or Jammu may embrace such a vision of its place in the state that it is not acceptable to the other and New Delhi has to intervene.

All these possibilities can become sharper if Pakistan

succeeds in its changed tactics in promoting trouble in India. It is not only supporting jehadi groups more openly by releasing some of their most virulent leaders from prison. It is also adding Hindu religious institutions in India to its list of targets in Kashmir. The aim obviously is to exacerbate Hindu-Muslim relations in India, which can have consequences in Jammu and Kashmir. The game has not succeeded so far, a shown by the election, but some success in future cannot be ruled out. However, these were not the issues before the state in the election. The issues was how to make the state a stable democracy within the Indian Union, and no party is now visible in the state which is opposed to this objective and also can win an election by itself or in combination with other parties. This is the perspective in which the result of the election is to be judged, not in terms of the tussle which took place between the Congress and PDP over the forming of the coalition between them, and because of which some newspapers hastily described the election as a failure.

But that does not mean we should agree to a plebiscite now. Whatever the reasons or circumstances in which India agreed to hold one, they were demolished by Pakistan, in the manner explained earlier, by violating the conditions laid down by the United Nations for holding it. Apart from that, however, there is no reason for applying a principle to India which has been repeatedly rejected by the United Nations. The world body, particularly the General Assembly has held more than once that self-determination is a principle which applies to the determination of the future of a former possession of the colonial powers, and not to any part of a sovereign country which is recognised as such by the United Nations by the act of admitting it to the UN as an independent country. Were separation by self-determination to become a universal principle in the UN system, it would apply to many countries, and then India could consider its application to India. A solution of the problem by dividing Kashmir along the LoC, advocated by some, is also possible only by agreement between the two countries, and apart from its impracticality on other counts it has been made inapplicable by its rejection by Pakistan.

With the outcome of this election democracy has regained much of the ground it had been loosing in the state since the very first fully democratic election was held in it as a condition for the acceptance of the accession by New Delhi in 1947. The earliest election in the state had not only introduced it to the ways of democracy. It had also vindicated the faith of the first Chief Minister, Sheikh Abdullah, in the secular future of the state and his economic vision. But the process soon became a prisoner of the political exigencies imposed upon the state by the perfidy of Pakistan and the cold war objectives of the United States. This cloud was lifted for a time in the late 1970s and the early 1980s, when democratic commitments re-asserted themselves both in the country and in the state, and in Kashmir it was lifted further when Farooq Abdullah, standing on a secular platform, battled successfully against so formidable an opponent as India's Prime Minister then, Mrs Indira Gandhi, whose platform had strong communal overtones in that campaign. This success, and the affront to her power which was implicit in it, was perhaps one of the reasons why she dismissed Farooq and his government soon afterwards. But thereafter democracy began to be undermined again when the National Conference in Srinagar and successive governments in New Delhi, each pleading its own political compulsions, derailed democracy in the state. In the mid-1980s Farooq Abdullah first created and then destroyed the chance of recovery, and a weak leadership in Delhi could do little to prevent him.

Communalisation of electoral politics had always been a danger in the state, and as it seemed at the time it raised a threatening head when the state began to prepare for the last election of the 1980s. Ghulam Mohammad Bhat, an able and effective leader of the frankly communal party, Jamaat-

I-Islami, succeeded in bringing communally inclined voters together under the umbrella of a Muslim United Front (MUF) and posed what looked like the biggest electoral threat the National Conference had faced till then. But instead of facing it with his own well proven electoral strength, Farooq Abdullah manipulated the electoral process to deny the Front even that much space to which it was entitled by the support it was able to muster by legitimate electoral means. As subsequent events were to show, neither was the MUF strong enough to defeat the National Conference nor was G.M. Bhatt's personality or programme entirely inimical to the state's larger interests and its accession to India. If Farooq had not cheated MUF out of its due share of seats, which was in any case much less than the legitimate share of the National Conference, the contribution of both leaders and their parties to the politics of the state probably would have been very different from and much better than it came to be.

Taking full advantage of the prostrate people of the state and their disenchantment with New Delhi's and Srinagar's professions of democracy, and playing instead upon the religious sentiments of the Muslims of the state, Pakistan succeeded in sidetracking the admirably secular political and economic struggle begun in Kashmir in the early 1950s by the National Conference. Instead the state became embroiled in a competition between India and Pakistan to show who could create more havoc, and MUF slipped into the fold of the separatists in the Hurriyat conglomerate. This gave the "Farooq family" further scope for convincing Delhi that Farooq was India's only hope in Kashmir, and therefore New Delhi must not look too closely at how the National Conference won elections. The result was as bad as could be expected.

It is from this pit that the electoral process in the state had to be lifted before the voter could be persuaded to believe that the Indian Constitution gave him all the rights of a voter in a democracy to elect a government of his choice. The task, difficult in any case because of the communal frenzy Pakistan had whipped up, was made much more so when the Pakistan-based militants turned their well proven prowess as terrorists upon voters. Before polling began in October, they declared that anyone found taking part in the election would be shot, and they backed up the threat with deadly attacks on polling stations and staff. No one was left in any doubt that the staff could hold elections and the people could vote only at serious and clear risk to their lives.

Yet both chose to face the risk. Assisted, no doubt, by the elaborate security at hand but driven mostly by their desire to assert their democratic rights, the people came out in appreciable numbers to vote. Unfortunately they could not do so in some urban concentrations, particularly in Srinagar, which had become the strongholds of armed militancy, and since these were densely populated areas, the overall turn out of voters was affected in parts of Kashmir. Yet the overall turn out was a respectable 45 per cent and even in Kashmir there were areas which registered above 60 per cent polling. This restoration and vindication of the electoral process was the first and main aim of the election, and it was met. The Central Election Commission helped by setting up polling booths within or close to disturbed areas so that the voter may not be exposed to avoidable risk, a device which could have been useful in the disturbed areas of Gujarat also but somehow was not used by the Election Commission there, thus creating room for avoidable controversy.

In the run up to the elections in Kashmir there was sufficient friction on display between the two main contenders in the valley, the National Conference on one side and the People's Democratic Party on the other, between the Congress and BJP in Jammu, and between the two electoral allies in the valley, the PDP and the Congress, to fuel media speculation on two counts : that the Congress and PDP would fall out over the share of each in the coalition government they were expected to set up, and second that the usual conflict of ambitions between Srinagar and New Delhi over control of the Kashmir government would flare up again. There was indeed some squabbling between the PDP and the Congress over who should hold the post of the Chief Minister in the coalition government. Chances of acrimony between the state government and the Union Home Minister also increased when, as the first step in the "healing touch" he had promised to apply to the people of the state, Mufti Mohammad Sayeed released some prisoners whom the Union Home Ministry regarded as a threat to security. But both problems were sorted out within days of their surfacing. BJP refrained from embarrassing the Congress during the elections in Gujarat by blaming it for being a party to the release of militants in Kashmir. The Congress and PDP agreed they would hold the post of the Chief Minister by turn and the Congress president, Sonia Gandhi, agreed to let the PDP have the first turn, a decision, taken in the face of strong opposition by senior leaders in the party, a fact which instantly raised her own standing in the country for statesmanship.

On the other side also, New Delhi and Srinagar agreed to set up a joint committee to screen releases. The Congress agreed to a screening committee, and the Chief Minister ordered that almost fifty persons who had been release without such screening should be re-arrested. (*The Tribune*, 29.11.2002) The state government also turned its attention more towards a more important healing touch, to curb the tendency of the security forces to take needlessly harsh and insensitive steps in the name of security. More important in the long run, the improvement in the political climate in the state as a result of the successful election, made it possible for the Union Home Minister and Deputy Prime Minister, Mr L.K. Advani, to announce a step which Mohammad Sayeed, now the state Chief Minister and Home Minister, had promised in his election campaign, that he would persuade the Union Government to open political discussions with various sections of political opinion in the state. Mr Advani announced in Jammu on December 27 that he would soon start a dialogue with "elected representatives and others." Among the others he included "those who have not participated in the elections" if they wanted to have discussions with New Delhi.

This last little caveat has placed the Hurriyat into an even more piquant situation than it was facing already. Mr Mohammad Sayeed welcomed Mr Advani's offer of talks, including talks with "those who have not participated in the elections." He considered this to be acceptance of " the state government's major demand for initiating an unconditional dialogue". He said no group or organisation should refuse to make a positive response, and "there is no role of the gun." But would the Hurriyat respond positively ? It had insisted over the years that it would negotiate with the Union Government only in a tripartite format, with Pakistan represented at the talks. The Union Government has insisted for equally long that while it is agreeable to discussing the future of Kashmir with Pakistan in a bilateral format, it does not see a place for Pakistan in a discussion between the government of the Indian Union and people of the state who are citizens of India. (*Hindustan Times*, December 30, 2002.) In a separate statement a few days later he specifically excluded from the ambit of talks those who, as he put it, considered themselves to be spokesmen on behalf of Pakistan. He did not name Hurriyat in that description but left a question hanging in the air : would he apply the label to the Hurriyat because of its insistence on Pakistan's presence at talks between Indian citizens ?

From the time when the Hurriyat began to show an interest in taking a delegation to Pakistan a couple of years ago, it has been caught in a game invented by Pakistan. Until lately, the Hurriyat had failed to see that in this game it would be a pawn, not a player. It failed because through most of its early and formative years it had been Pakistan's political platform in Kashmir, the political arm of most of the underground militants who were waging an armed war against India with the active support of the Pakistan army. Therefore, it did not look critically at Pakistan's manoevures. Those were the years in which Hurriyat leaders during their visits to Delhi became, and were happy to be, prize exhibits at functions at the Pakistan High Commission, particularly on Pakistan's national day, while their distance from India's Republic Day celebrations and other such Indian occasions was conspicuous, particularly when Geelani was its president. India too then kept the Hurriyat at arm's length while dealing with other Kashmiri groups. But this suited Pakistan as it tried to convince the people of Kashmir that the Hurriyat had no influence with New Delhi and they had no alternative to the jehad waged by heavily armed militants pushed into Kashmir by Pakistan, even though their non-Kashmiri persona grated on the nerves of Kashmiris. But in Hurriyat's own elections in 2001 to choose the organisation's next president, Geelani was defeated by Mirwaiz Umar Farooq, son of the preceding Mirwaiz or Imam of Srinagar's biggest mosque, who had been assassinated by suspected Pakistani militants because they thought he was inclined towards India. After his defeat Geelani began to denounce his opponents as secular because they did not see the "Kashmir problem" as religious.

Under the new president Hurriyat was slowly succeeding in doing two things, in rescuing Kashmir's own interests from the coils of Pakistan's confrontation with India, and in carving out a role for the Hurriyat as a constructive factor both in the affairs of Jammu and Kashmir and as a possible interlocutor for India and Pakistan, talking to each in turn instead of both together. But this did not suit Pakistan. As a political entity based in the soil and society of Kashmir, where priorities are changing in response to the growing desire among the people for peace and order, Hurriyat could become a less reliable instrument for Pakistan than militants nurtured in the currents of jehad which are sweeping through

Pakistan.

Therefore Pakistan, with the help of Geelani and such non-Kashmiri militant organisations as are thoroughly committed to Pakistan, began to run down Hurriyat's proposal that India should allow it to visit Pakistan, which Pakistan now began to describe as a useless exercise. This means that while on the one hand the Hurriyat lost ground in Kashmir among those who did not subscribe to Geelani's hard line, on the other hand its less extreme members who were strong enough to defeat Geelani in the election for the post of president of the organisation found Pakistan moving away from them. Pakistan also complicated Hurriyat's role by insisting that if it visited Pakistan at all it could do so only at the invitation of Pakistan, as the sole representative of Kashmir, only to mediate between India and Pakistan, and for the sole purpose of setting up a tripartite meeting between India, Pakistan and Kashmir. This was the role it assigned to the Hurriyat in a statement dated December 2, 2001, and repeatedly cited by Pakistan as a definitive formulation of its position regarding the Hurriyat.

It said, "In order to enable the representatives of the Kashmiri people to participate in the dialogue" (with India, which the statement proposed in an earlier paragraph) " the Government of Pakistan extends an invitation to the Executive Committee of the All Parties Hurriyat Conference, the leader of the Kashmiri freedom struggle, for consultations to prepare the ground for a tripartite process of negotiations ....". After many weeks in internal discussions, Hurriyat issued a statement early in the following Febraury resuming the new president's policy of at least appearing to disengage from Pakistan's view of the role of the Hurriyat's role. Its statement was silent on its earlier insistence on a tripartite meeting, although demanded also by Pakistan in its own statement , and did not use any of the derogatory references to India with which the statement by Pakistan is peppered. It described the Kashmir problem as "political" in character, not "religious", and did not claim to be the sole representative of Kashmir. But that does not exclude it from groups which did not participate in the recent election, or those claimed by Pakistan to be its invitees or, as Mr Advani said in a statement on December 27, 2002, are " proxies of Pakistan" because, in talking to Pakistan "we don't need intermediaries." On the other hand Mufti Mohammad Sayeed, while saying that the details of the talks had yet to be worked out, implied that he favoured the inclusion of those who " do not believe in the state's accession to the Union of India." (*The Hindu*, December 29, 2002).

Therefore, while Mr. Advani and Mufti Mohammad Sayeed have opened the door for talks between Srinagar and New Delhi, it is not yet clear how the two will get over the differences between them on who should be included in or excluded from the talks. An answer may be found in a method suggested by Mufti Sayeed in an interview to *Hindustan Times* of January 7, 2003, backed as it is by the stature given him by the recent election. Affirming "complete understanding between the central and state governments", he suggested, "The first step should be to talk to the representatives in the state assembly", that is those who took part in the election — and got elected— "and then engage those who do not believe in the accession" of the state to India, a description which covers many who did not take part in the election, in fact opposed it, but do not belong to the Hurriyat, and certainly not to that part of the Hurriyat which is closer to Geelani than to those such as Mirwaiz Umar Farooq.

Hurriyat's claim that it represents Kashmir has also been undermined by more recent developments within Kashmir. Hurriyat has figured often as an interlocutor favoured most by some non-official groups in India, and of course, by its supporters in Pakistan. But its claim to be representative of the people of the valley, undermined earlier by the better performance of the National Conference in elections, has now been even more clearly undermined by the performance of the PDP in the valley itself in the election last year. Secondly, the statement by Pakistan, quoted above, has more clearly conferred on the Hurriyat the status of an intervener most favoured by Pakistan, and therefore exposed to the disqualification pronounced by Mr Advani against those Kashmiris who appear as special advocates of Pakistan. Thirdly, the role the Congress might play in deciding whose participation in the talks might be supported by the Mufti government will probably not go in favour of the Hurriyat. The Hurriyat has also been alienated from public sentiment by the suspected association of Geelani with those who assassinated the most popular single leader of the Hurriyat, Abdul Ghani Lone. His son, Sajjad Lone, clearly implied their guilt, and that of the more pro-Pakistan members of the Hurriyat. His crime in their eyes appears to have been his talks with Indian leaders who were searching for answers to Kashmir questions.

Recognition of this reality is reflected in the statement by the Hurriyat's former chairman, Mirwaiz Umar Farooq, on December 29, 2002. In an interview with *The Hindu* of that date he said Hurriyat was willing to give up a position to which it had held for a long time, that it would talk to New Delhi only after it had been allowed to go and talk to Pakistan first. He said he was willing to reverse the sequence. This also is a non-starter, of course, because India and Pakistan will talk to each other only when the direct equation between them allows both of them to do so. It obviously does not so long as India insists that this bilateral dialogue can begin only when the traffic of raiders from the Pakistan side of the Line of Control declines significantly, and Pakistan insists that it has already done what it could do and there is nothing more it can do.

Even when the talks between New Delhi and Srinagar do take place, as they probably will, they will face an initial hurdle left over by an unfortunate spat between them three years ago regarding the powers of the state government and the extent of the jurisdiction of the Union on the exercise of those powers by the state. This can be removed only if both sides take the statesmanlike decision to focus more on the content than of the context of two key words : "autonomy" and "devolution". The former word can prove to be a mine-field, the latter a pathway to agreement. The mine-field was laid by both sides with equal shortsightedness, the pathway can only be laid by both with farsightedness.

In one of his fits of indiscretion, Farooq Abdullah appears to have gone back on an assurance he had given to the Government of India that while the state assembly must discuss the popular demand for "autonomy", it would not raise any very specific demands until he had consulted New Delhi. Instead he confronted New Delhi with a fully worked out and overloaded charter of demands, embodied in a Report on Autonomy which his cabinet had already put through the state assembly. New Delhi's response was also ill-tempered and hasty. Instead of reasoning with him and explaining what could be considered and what could not be for the time being, an approach to which he has never failed to respond when his ego and temper have cooled, New Delhi brusquely rejected the report and, as it were, asked him to find his way home.

In the process, both sides overlooked the fact that in 1975-76 Sheikh Abdullah and Mrs Indira Gandhi had signed an agreement that, if requested by the state assembly, India would review any extensions of New Delhi's jurisdiction over the state which had been effected during the years that the Sheikh was in prison. Both Srinagar and New Delhi would have been better off if they had gone back to that agreement instead of Srinagar throwing new demands on the table and New Delhi throwing them out of the window. In renewed discussions in the new situation the Mufti government would not have asked for the moon because its partner, the

Congress would not have backed unreasonable demands. New Delhi would not have spurned practicable demands because that would have been opposed by some of BJP's partners in the NDA government, who favour grant of more powers to state governments.

A way out exists through three gates. First, Srinagar must realise that the greater the autonomy it demands from New Delhi the greater will be the autonomy demanded by Jammu and Ladakh from Srinagar. Second, New Delhi must respond to the new situation created by the recent election. Just as the Indian military has shown Pakistan can never wrest the state by force, the voters have shown Pakistan cannot get it by political subversion either. Therefore both can revert to the wisdom of the remark by a former Prime Minister of India, Mr Narasimha Rao, that short of secession the sky is the limit for the powers the state can have. Third, both should revert to the enhanced "devolution" envisaged in any honest interpretation of the Indira-Sheikh agreement.

That word is limitlessly flexible and can accommodate whatever quantum of devolution New Delhi and Srinagar can agree upon. Any apprehension Srinagar may have that what New Delhi may devolve upon J&K today it may withdraw tomorrow can be firmly set at rest by writing the agreed devolution into the Union Constitution and also into such J&K constitution as the state may still have under the agreed devolution.This would give the devolution the same constitutional protection from Srinagar's point of view that the state's accession to India has from New Delhi's point of view. It would also eliminate the risk that either on its own or at the prodding of interested third parties the state may contest any action of the Union Government on the ground that it is inconsistent with whatever meaning the word "autonomy" might have acquired by that time because of constitutional practices in other countries, just as a notion is being advocated in the recent literature on federalism that the constituent states of a federation should be free to evolve their own place in the foreign policy of the federation. (see the author's articles "Sovereignty of Federations", I and II, in *The Hindu*, December 9, 10, 2002) Such squabbling can re-awaken the ghost of "plebiscite" which the United Nations itself, not India, buried in 1957. For example, the word "autonomy" can mean different things to Chinese and Tibetan leaders, and different things in different contexts. Many countries would watch the differences with interest. It is true "autonomy" of sorts has been conceded, and by that name, to some special regions of some other states of the Indian Union. But they have also provided precedents for the safety of the content which the word has in those cases.

However, each of these possible ways of coping with the issue will also have to cope with the pressures of coalitional politics within J&K and electoral politics in the rest of the country, which will be quite hot throughout 2003 because of the assembly elections in several Indian states. The election has shown that there is not much left of what was earlier thought to be a source of political instability, that is the political separatism preached by the Hurriyat. In fact its influence has been shown to be much less than was anticipated, except in some very densely populated parts of Srinagar and a few other urban concentrations, in which the Mirwaiz has political influence, and in some border areas where Geelani has some. A higher voter turn out might have increased the vote share of the National Conference, the PDP and the Congress, none of whom can be called a separatist party in any case, but would not have changed the seat share very much, and that is relevant to the force a party's voice may have in the legislature. Besides, the coalition between the Congress and PDP might be put under some strain as domestic and national politics become more shrill in the coming months.

There are some strong reasons for expecting that the Congress and PDP will do their best to stay together. Neither can find a better partner than the other among today's electoral parties. Nor is there any other party which can make up a majority by breaking away some splinters from the Congress and or the PDP. Not even the National Conference, though it is the largest single party. Nor has PDP much prospect of finding better company at the national level, at least until after the next parliamentary election, than the NDA. Who it finds then will depend upon the results of that election. But no visible combination is likely to have an adverse effect upon the accession of J&K to India.

But that cannot be said of some lesser issues, which can affect the temperature and stability of relations between coalition partners in Srinagar. Issues like the status of Jammu and Ladakh within a unified J&K, the severity of measures against the residual militancy which is indigenous to Kashmir, or against infiltrators from across the border, or relations between the two sides of the state, or the resulting relations between India and Pakistan. Disagreements on these issues might or might not bring down the coalition between the Congress and PDP. But they could affect its efficacy in governance and thence its longer term acceptability in the state. It is possible that such uncertainties will be resolved only over a period of time.

However, the election in the Indian side of J&K has had an interesting even if indirect ripple effect on the Pakistan side, as is confirmed by some angry press comments in the first week of January this year by Sardar Abdul Qayyum, a former President of the government of what goes by the misnomer of Azad (or "independent") Kashmir, the part of Kashmir which is on the Pakistan side of the Line of Control and like Pakistan itself has often been under military rule. If one remembers correctly, Mr Qayyum is the same gentleman who, when he was President of the Azad Kashmir government, was threatened with trial for treason by the Pakistan government for stepping out of line once too often. Lately he has been president of the "Kashmir Committee", set up by the Pakistan government as an additional channel for communication with Azad Kashmir, bypassing the local government. (It is not to be confused with a non-official committee of the same name set up in India by independent groups for dialogue with the separatists and other opposition groups in J&K)

The term of the Kashmir Committee expired in the middle of January, 2003, and Mr Qayyum had to step down. But before doing so he fired a salvo on the powers that be in Pakistan. In a press statement he said that his committee had been set up "to create a friendly atmosphere between India and Pakistan, which would help them resolve the Kashmir row." But the "traditional bureaucratic system did not let the committee work effectively.... the committee was an unconventional entity but the bureaucracy did not let it work effectively." The Pakistan *Daily Times* reported that Qayyum said the next committee must get legal cover and its members should be strong and popular politicians who would work for Kashmir. He hoped that the present bureaucratic system would not create any problems for the new committee. The paper also commented editorially on January 4, " Sardar Qayyum's committee has died because no one in it could agree with the changing international perspectives on the Kashmir jihad... Sardar Saheb was pilloried by the press for blaspheming against the jihadi militias, then he was hauled over the coals for suggesting that Pakistan should consider a solution based on the Line of Control (LoC) .... The onus of formulating a new stance on Kashmir in these circumstances was too much (for the Committee) because its members were either too scared or too hide-bound to accept new realities, especially as the jihadi and religious leaders were excoriating Sardar Qayyum for heresy in the Kashmir Cause."

The Impact on India

For close upon half a century there was a debate in India between two schools of thought about the best route for reaching a solution of this "problem", whatever it might really be. One school said " solve your problem with Pakistan and the 'Kashmir problem' will go away." The other said " solve your problem with the people of Kashmir and the 'Pakistan problem' will go away, no matter who created it and why." This election has effectively ended that debate. It has been replaced by the realisation that "Kashmir" is no more a problem than are many other parts of this vast and varied country. Those 'problems' were better resolved when they were handled fairly and truly democratically, such as the problems of linguistic, ethnic, political or communal 'separatism', than when we played tricks with the people concerned. So can the 'Kashmir problem' be solved, and then the 'Pakistan problem' will also fall into place, with or without any outside 'assistance.'

That is because this election has shown, not just again but more convincingly than anything had shown before, that the 'problem' is not with the political status of the state but with the status of the democratic rights of the people, the right to elect a government of their choice and to change it when they decide to, and the right to have at least as decent governance as most people have in this part of the world. The voter shed few tears, as he would have done some years ago, over the election being held under the overall jurisdiction of the 'Indian' Election Commission instead of under the exclusive jurisdiction of a state election commission as it would have been at one time. But he was glad they were fair, even if the extent of their being free was curtailed by the activities of the militants, whose threats lowered the voter turn out, and some partisanship by the state security forces which became an additional blot. But impartial assessments indicate that a higher voter turn out would not have materially changed the political composition of the outcome.

The election result has also overtaken another debate, on the question who should New Delhi talk to in Kashmir. To the Abdullah government, which the Hurriyat claims had discredited itself in the eyes of the people ? To the Hurriyat itself, which according to other people represents only itself? To other separatists, and including or excluding the violent ones ? Now that there is a legislature in place which has been elected by a process widely recognised as fair, a government elected by it obviously has the first claim to be recognised as the prime interlocutor and must have a say in choosing other participants in the dialogue. It is no longer necessary for the government of India to send reconnaissance teams on its own to scout for others or to assess the representativeness of other claimants to a place at the table. Therefore the election has nullified the advice Mirwaiz Umar Farooq gave to the Government of India when, in the interview to *The Hindu* quoted above, he said the Government must decide who it should talk to.

But the most beneficial result for India as a whole as also for the state is the increased credibility, both at home and abroad, of India's intentions to restore democracy to the state as the first essential step, and then to go to further steps about the rights of the state, including devolution of more powers to it, and then to go on to negotiations with Pakistan for a final settlement, as soon as external circumstances for doing so improved, notably cessation of terrorism from across the border. This change has made it much easier for India to hold on to its position about the issue at stake. Otherwise it would have been more difficult for India to resist any American desire that India should go soft on Pakistan so that America might get a better deal from Pakistan in America's fight against the Al Qaeda remnants entrenched in the frontier areas of Pakistan and across the border in Afghanistan. There is clearly a clash here between Indian and American priorities in this matter, and the result of the election in J & K has made it easier for India to press its own priorities.

The Impact on Pakistan

The elections in J & K have a far reaching political meaning for Pakistan, in parallel with the military meaning of the India-Pakistan wars of 1947-48, 1965, 1971, and the Kargil conflict in 1998. This political meaning was clear though it was understood only slowly by those who needed to understand it quickest, that subversion, whether in the name of religion or self-determination, and terrorism no matter how much assisted by other countries, will fail just as military means had failed earlier. In fact the more that the militancy in Kashmir was seen to have a foreign face the more it lost ground, and lost it faster than it had been gained. The foreign faced militancy split in the early months of 2001, and barely eighteen months later it stood disowned in this election by the majority of the people of Kashmir. The conflict between India and Pakistan will be resolved, whenever or if ever it is, through patient negotiations in which agreements reached at every and any stage are honoured at all stages, regardless of changes in regime in either country. Towards that end, Pakistan should now accept the advice publicly given it by its most trusted friend, China, that when an important problem proves more difficult to solve, a beginning should be made with less difficult ones. Their solution improves the chances of solutions being found for the most difficult also.

Finally, the *Elections in Gujarat*, and their impact on Kashmir, India, and Pakistan.

Unlike the elections in Kashmir, which had a leg in the affairs of both India and Pakistan, the ones in Gujarat were primarily the state's internal affair and therefore does not have to figure much in Kashmir perspectives. But they do have certain aspects which relate to Kashmir and some which relate to India's relations with Pakistan via the relations between Hindus and Muslims in India.

In our worry about Pakistan's attempts to try to manipulate the communal divide in the rest of India to its advantage in Kashmir we should not overlook five facts. First, although Muslims of many nationalities, from Algeria to Chechenya, have been active in the terrorism let lose in Kashmir, very few if any have been seen there from among Indian Muslims. Second, by and large Indian Muslims have not publicly voiced any opposition to the Indian position on Kashmir. They have been critical, if even that, of the human rights aspects of security operations, which have been a matter of concern for many Indians of many points of view. Third, although the ugliest scenes witnessed in the communal rioting in Gujarat, whether by Hindus or Muslims, had been enacted before the elections in Jammu and Kashmir, they did not figure much in the debates within J&K either before or during or after the elections in J&K, whether in the Hindu majority province of Jammu or the Muslim majority province of Kashmir. Fourth, Moulvi Abbas Ansari, a senior leader of Hurriyat, protested publicly when the United Jehad Council of Pakistan, which is in overall control of the Pakistan government's agenda of terrorism against Kashmir, demanded that Kashmiri Muslims should boycott the election in the state. "Who are they", he asked, "to dictate to us what we should do and what we should not?" (*Hindustan Times*, 3.7.02) In a statement to the press the United Jehad Council had said "If the Hurriyat fails in its duties, the *mujahideen*" (the Council's word for terrorists) "will not be mere spectators. We will take the matter into our own hands and will do all to enforce a poll boycott". Fifth, Sajjad Lone, son of Abdul Ghani Lone, the slain top leader of the Hurriyat, denounced the Pakistan-based militants as deserters at a large public rally in Kashmir and said the people of Kashmir were not ready to take dictates from deserters across the border. (*The Hindu*, 5.8.02) What follows from these facts is that while there is much that India needs to worry about regarding Pakistan's activities among Indian Muslims, its impact on electoral politics in Kashmir is not among them.

However, that does not mean India can be complacent

about the state of relations between Hindus and Muslims in the rest of the country. If they continue to deteriorate they can influence the climate in Kashmir as well. This can be gravely to the detriment of India as a whole, and equally to the detriment of the interests of Muslims as well as non-Muslims, even if it be the case that in the long run the interests of the Muslim may get harmed more than the interests of non-Muslims. Already it can be said that there is a mood of sullen alienation today between India's Hindus and Muslims which will take longer to cure than the anger which divided them in the decade following the mid-1940s. That anger was like a storm which came and went. The present sullen mood is like a spell of oppressive weather which refuses to go away.

This is connected with the India-Pakistan relations in three ways. First, it encourages Pakistan to continue to believe that it can find agents among Indian Muslims who would be willing to carry out its bidding. Second it encourages Pakistan to continue to indulge in those activities against India which are sustained by its hope of finding suitable agents for carrying them out. Third, it makes many a Hindu more suspicious of his Muslim neighbour whenever a Muslim is suspected to be behind any event which hurts India's security, and that unfortunately happens all too often, both in India, which matters most, and in the form of events in the countries of this region which also ring bells in the Indian mind. The suspect is then seen as an agent for Pakistan, and Pakistan becomes more confident of finding more of such agents. The poison of communalism in India is then made more deadly by the poison of India-Pakistan relations.

This provokes understandable resentment among Indian Muslims as they perceive that they are being asked to stand up again and again and take oaths of loyalty to India. But the resentment is only as justified as the perception is correct, and neither is entirely so. Indian Muslims do not need to convince Hindus. But they need to do what it takes to disabuse Pakistan's mind of its hope and expectation that the few Indian Muslims who are caught playing Pakistan's games are only the tip of an iceberg. They are not, and this will dawn on Pakistan only when Muslim opinion in India becomes unmistakable. This will happen when this opinion is clearly heard to be at one with the voice of the rest of India whenever Pakistan's actions clearly go against India's legitimate interests. Not only heard in India, but in Pakistan, and in the rest of the Muslim world. Pakistan may or may not be worried about the voice of Indian Muslims as such. But it will be worried when it is heard in the Islamic world, in which Indian Muslims count for as much as Pakistan does, especially when it is heard as part of India's voice.

The mutual alienation between Hindus and Muslims makes parochialism a more volatile element in nationalism because a non-Muslim Indian may it as his patriotic duty to smell out suspects under every bed, and more often than not he claims to have fished out a Muslim. Often this is a case of mistaken identity, and more so in very recent years because of the high power and persuasive international imagery of terrorists in Islamic clothes. But unfortunately even in the Indian context the identification is also correct often enough to hide the mistakes made out of a bias against Muslims, and those who are correctly identified are all too often traceable to Pakistan. Each instance of this kind becomes a setback to the confidence level between Muslim and non-Muslim neighbours in India. Indian Muslims are not alone in being the victims of this complex, as Muslims of different Islamic sects know to their cost in several Muslim majority countries, and in Pakistan more than in many other Islamic countries because of the sectarian wars there between different sects of Muslims.

The power of such prejudices was also proved to the cost of many hundreds of Sikhs when disturbances broke out between Hindus and Sikhs in Punjab and the support bases of some Sikh organisations involved in them were traced to

Pakistan. I suspect that this perverted nationalism, which is different from religious communalism, also played a part in the outcome of the Gujarat elections and the barbarity which accompanied them, because many preceding events had sensitised the Gujarati voter to the dangerous potential of Pakistan. Probably the purely electoral outcome there was influenced more by the more conventional strategies of electoral battles, such as finding and keeping the right allies, choosing the right constituency for every candidate according to his and the constituency's social profile, choosing a credible leader of the party's campaign, and getting it going at the right time.

Of course this can complicate the Jammu & Kashmir scene as well, where the valley is predominantly Muslim and Jammu correspondingly Hindu, and the eviction of Kashmiri Pandits from the valley remains a bleeding wound. This does not mean that there is much substance in either of two dire prophecies that are sometimes made, whether out of mischief or a misreading of history or out of mistaken perceptions of the present. The first is that the Hindu mind being as suspicious as some suspect it to be, and Indian Muslims being as conspicuous a minority as they are, the latter are doomed to float precariously for ever on an ocean of Hindu prejudice. The second is that the Muslims are a large enough minority to break up India again if they are not given their due. Both prophecies are absurd. India was not broken up in 1947 by the strength of Indian Muslims but by the perfidious alliance which British imperial interests made with the demand for Pakistan.. India is far too strong today to be broken up by any updated perfidy of the same kind.

And as the example of the Sikhs and many other minorities has shown, once the cloud of misperceptions is blown away by mutual efforts, all kinds of minorities and majorities, whether religious, linguistic, societal, racial, can live together in comfort, and India has better examples of that to show than many other countries. But if there is a grain of probability in either prophecy, the cure lies in the domestic politics of the country. For this reason one turns now to some suggestions for correcting some angularities in Indian public opinion which make us see a bigger danger than is warranted in every signal that something is amiss. If such exaggerated sensitivity is carried too far, it can make India more vulnerable to the damage a country or society inflicts upon itself if it suspects every innocent person to be a thief because he looks different. But if a sense of proportion prevails soon enough, the emerging perspectives on many things, as in this case Kashmir, will become stronger and clearer than they have almost ever been, better though they are even today than any which have been seen since the early 1950s.

The first thing wrong in our national psyche is that we get over excited by every surprise. Particularly by an unpleasant surprise, and all the more so if it can be used against the government of the day, whichever the government might be. A constantly agitated public remains constantly unstable, unpredictable, at all times unable to find the right remedies or to focus on them when found. It sees a mountainous enemy in every unfamiliar molehill, and by the time the enemy is correctly sized up people are too tired to react or have moved on the next oversized headline.

The two issues most vulnerable to this angularity relate to Kashmir and Pakistan. At first the elections in Kashmir aroused expectations that they would solve every problem there. But within a few days the solid contribution they could make to far reaching restoration of democracy was forgotten and gloom set in over delays in the choice of the Chief Minister of the coalition because of a tussle between the Congress and the PDP.

There is justified sorrow over the loss of innocent lives in Kashmir as the terrorists hit "soft targets" , which means people who have nothing to do with the aims of jehad. But there is not enough recognition that despite the occasional and tragic (but often avoidable) death of young Indian soldiers, Pakistan has lost its second game with the gun. Having lost the first, which it played with its regular armed forces, it began a second, with the mujahideen, only to discover that whatever such beasts may be able to do with unsuspecting persons on the road they are loosing support among the people as the elections have shown. They cannot deliver the state to Pakistan, and without hope of doing that they can only inflict pin pricks. Nasty though these may be, and involve tragic loss of innocent lives in some cases, they pose no threat to India's solidarity and strength.

The tragedies of the casualties we suffer in Kashmir or loss of effective control over parts of the state must be stopped as soon as possible. But they do not pose a more serious threat to lives and the country's interests than what is happening in large parts of Andhra and the whole of the neighboring tribal belt. The difference in the public's concern about the two shows how the public's perceptions can be distorted by some mental attitudes. The policy consequences of such distortions were brought home to the country by the media treatment of the hijacking of an Indian airlines plane on a flight from Kathmandu.

Pakistan is indeed playing a dangerous new game by directing fedayeen attacks to religion-sensitive targets or gatherings of people, be they only as small as a railway comparment can carry. But these also can succeed only to the extent that they are allowed to by the state of India's public mind. Such attacks are not half as destructive as the public's reactions and counter reactions can be. The resulting alienation between Hindus and Muslims can also be dangerous, even if not half as lethal for India as rabid opinion holds them to be. But the best remedy for that lies in the public mind. Such tricks cannot separate people who do not wish to be separated.

In the same category are the wholly unfounded fears in the public mind that Indian decisions regarding Kashmir and relations with Pakistan are being determined by "foreign pressures." There has never been a time when there has been less "pressure" on India, on behalf of Pakistan or any other country, whether regarding Kashmir or any other issue related to Pakistan, and the election in Kashmir has made a more important contribution to that than any other event relating to Kashmir.

Diplomatic counsels can be wholly shut out only by a country which wholly shuts out the world, and probably not even then. They can "determine" a country's decisions only if the country has no other options, and probably not even then as, as Myanmar has discovered. But India has more options today than at any time since it became independent, and at no time has it used with greater skill and sophistication or with better results. There may be two opinions on whether it could have used them still better. But comparison with the past has been reassuring in the tactics used and the results obtained.

The consequence is that on the whole India has better relations with the world community as a whole than it has ever had, from America right round the world and back to America, via Europe, Russia, Cental Asia,West Asia, China, Japan.

Pakistan continues to be a sorry exception to that. But no source of "foreign pressure" has been able to come up with a single remedy for that which India has not tried. On the other hand the patronage other countries have extended to Pakistan, for their own various reasons and regardless of the effect on Pakistan, has pushed Pakistan closer to failure as a state. If in that lies an answer to the Indo-Pakistan problem, waiting patiently may yet be the best policy for India, whether in the Kashmir or a wider context. In the meantime India is being better defended, and more by its own resources, than at any time before. In most matters of external relations it can afford to wait. The internal depend upon its own will; the resources have never been better.

3

Assessment

Early, 2000

The general opinion in Jammu and Srinagar, particularly in the latter, is that the state entered a promising phase in 1996, as indicated by the extent of the participation in the elections held in that year. But this phase petered out because not enough effort was made to consolidate it. On the contrary some avoidable mistakes were made in the succeeding couple of years, and then some adverse consequences intervened in the wake of Kargil conflict. Otherwise the situation would have been much better than it is today.

If that is so, then the conclusion follows that the system which could yield such a phase despite all that had happened in the first half of the 1990s, when militancy and protest were at their highest, is basically sound and can fulfil its promise if mistakes are avoided, positive steps are taken promptly, and extraneous factors, like the Kargil conflict in the present, are dealt with properly. There were no insurmountable difficulties in the way of doing any of that in Jammu and Kashmir in the second half of the 1990s. Nor are there any now, and the situation is retrievable if there is the will to retrieve it.

This overview applies as much to the political as to the security, economic, societal, and administrative aspects of the present and recent situations in the state.

Political

There is a political vacuum in the state at present. The traditional leaders have lost their credibility. Effective alternatives are not visible yet. Some who aspire to be alternatives complain that the incumbent political leadership does not allow them to come up. But an aspirant who needs the incumbent's permission is obviously not yet ready for his aspirations. At the same time, while it is generally agreed that the present leadership remains better than those seeking to replace it, it is also agreed that the incumbent has lost much of his previous will, focus, energy, application. That is the essence of the vacuum.

On their part the leaders of the present government of the state allege that they are being let down by the present leadership in Delhi which, at its highest level, promises economic support but does not deliver it, or not in time, and its political support is also suspect. On the other hand New Delhi is not sure of the capabilities or even the intentions of the incumbent government in the state. The result is that no one is providing firm leadership to the state. This may also be true of some other states of India but they are not as vulnerable to external interventions.

What makes this drift more tragic is that perfectly competent people are available in J & K at many levels, in the academia, politics, the economy, the administration, but no one seems able any longer to build them into a coherent team with adequate support structures. There are some fresh faces and fresh initiatives, but in general there is a paucity of both.

The Chief Minister, Mr Farooq Abdullah, is trying to fill the vacuum with a demand for more autonomy for the state within the Indian Union. He has stepped up the demand in some recent statements, and it has now acquired more substance, edge, focus, with the release of the report of the state autonomy committee, which has recommended that the Union Government should roll back all the legislation which has extended the jurisdiction of the Union over the state much beyond the limits it had when J&K acceded to India. The justification claimed for the demand is that most of these extensions were made when Sheikh Mohammad Abdullah and other prominent leaders of public opinion in Kashmir were in prison.

It is open to question whether the people of the state are greatly agitated over the quantum of autonomy the state has or should have, compared to their concern over the safety of their lives and a reasonable livelihood. But there is no doubt that the demand has a history of relevance and legitimacy, and political complications can ensue if it is not considered rationally, systematically, and in time, without the baggage of past suspicions and emotions. There are reasons for saying so.

In the first place, although the state acceded to India with the full consent of the people it did so only with regard to three subjects, defence, external affairs, and communications, and some related matters. Some subsequent extensions of the Union's jurisdiction might also be popular, such as those of the Supreme Court, the Election Commission, the Comptroller and Auditor-General, but not all, and some might fail if subjected to a public poll.

Secondly, the agreement made in 1975 between Sheikh Abdullah and Mrs Gandhi conceded that the Union Government would review all such extensions as the state assembly may recommend for such a review. But action on the agreement was stalled by those in power in New Delhi by various means. Thirdly, the present leadership of Kashmir won the mandate of the people of Kashmir on the basis of an agenda which prominently included restoration of the autonomy.

But the demand for restoration of the original autonomy has become rather more controversial in recent years because of relations between some of the leaders of the (largely Muslim) region, the Kashmir Valley, and people who speak in the name of the two non-Kashmiri (and largely non-Muslim) regions, Jammu and Ladakh. The latter see the Union's jurisdiction over the state as their safeguard against excessive domination of the Kashmiri region and leaders over them.

That is probably the reason why at the time when the state autonomy committee was appointed to study the state's autonomy from (but within) the Union, another committee was also appointed to study the autonomy of the regions within the state. But while the state autonomy committee has already published a detailed report, which is currently the subject of some seminars backed by the state leadership, the report of the regional autonomy committee has not reached that status yet. Though a draft is under circulation, the Chief Minister says it is still being examined by an academic appointed by the government. In the meantime Jammu based intellectuals and academics are objecting to it on the ground that it envisages, among other things, division of Jammu, a Hindu majority region, into several regions of which some would have a Muslim majority.

There is potential here for controversy, which has already been flagged by the hitherto unexplained resignation of Dr. Karan Singh (son of the last Maharaja of J&K, who had signed the accession to India) as chairman of the state autonomy committee. He was succeeded Mr Ghulam Mohiudin Shah. If future dissension is to be forestalled, it is clearly necessary that the issue of autonomy should receive timely and open minded consideration, both in New Delhi and Srinagar, and in all three regions of the state of Jammu and Kashmir.

In the meantime electoral politics might also emerge from a possibility which has been half opened by the Chief Minister. He has publicly announced that he is willing to dissolve the legislative assembly and hold fresh elections, (that is about eighteen months before they are due) if those who boycotted the last elections would agree to take part in them. There are various views about his reasons for making this announcement : ranging from putting a lid on dissidence in his own party, to a desire to strengthen his hand in a possible dialogue with New Delhi over the autonomy demand, to a move for forestalling the possibility that his chances for winning may decline as he waits another year or more in office, to a sincere attempt to end the present political vacuum so that, under whoever may win, the state may get down to the many suspended tasks.

Some prominent Kashmiri leaders who have not been well disposed towards the accession to India have said in private that they would consider participating in the election, and elections to urban and rural local bodies which are due in mid-summer, if proper and open ended consultations were held first with all the state actors taking part, while participation by Pakistan could be considered later. This is also the opinion of some of the leaders of the Hurriyat, an umbrella organisation of groups which are opposed to the present government of J&K but do not necessarily demand secession from India. Until lately the Hurriyat had contact with and some influence over some of the militant groups but is losing this leverage with the militancy again becoming more strident. They feel that if the government, whether at the centre or in J&K, does not open a dialogue with them quite soon it will have no Kashmiri element left with whom it can do so. Panchayat elections have also been scheduled for the coming mid-summer, and although intended to be held on a non-party basis they too could indicate peoples' support for various points of view. They would also validate panchayats as an important vehicle of development at the grass roots. Some of those who boycotted the legislative elections seem agreeable to taking part in the the panchayat elections if they were held on a non-party basis, which the state government intends to do.

Security

It is generally agreed, particularly in Srinagar, that the security situation has deteriorated over the past year or so, and particularly since the Kargil conflict. The decision making powers in Pakistan have been stepping up the conflict as part of their strategy for drawing international attention to the "Kashmir dispute." Since the Kargil conflict they have had the added reason of trying to prove that they did not lose. But a more worrisome consequence is that the Indian security forces have not only had to retaliate harder, which is understandable, but in their more embattled mood have also begun again to violate human rights, as they used to do some years ago but had refrained from doing more recently. Much worse now is the behaviour of those former militants who have been absorbed into the security set up but constitute a special "task force".

The effect on public opinion in the state, and particularly in the valley, is what it should be expected to be, and there are many reports that Kashmiri youth have again become victims of lurements from across the border to come and be trained in wielding arms. Whereas the armed insurgency had at one time ceased to have many Kashmiri recruits and was largely the work of heavily armed "foreigners", that is people from "Azad Kashmir", Pakistan, and farther afield, now it has some Kashmiri infusion again, or from the Muslim majority border areas of the Jammu region, whether motivated by convictions or cash. On the other hand the foreign militant has also become shrewder : he makes himself less offensive to the local population than he used to do, even to Kashmiri Muslims.

The additional strain has started to take a toll of the morale, alertness, and efficiency of the security forces, and command and control within and between the different branches of them. The effect has escalated into some serious lapses in recent months though they had not been entirely absent earlier either. On the other hand the recent successes of the terrorists have added to their ferocity and firepower. At the political level some leaders of the Hurriyat, an umbrella organisation of Kashmiri opponents of the state government, feel that the militancy is getting difficult for them.

The militancy has also had some encouragement from an unexpected quarter. It had been assumed by the authorities that the militants would earn the disapproval of the people if they harmed the infrastructure, such as power, and thus added to the misery of the people. But as explained by a person, himself of security, the infrastructure is so poor already, and power is given as an example again, that some further damage to it does not affect the people much while it dramatises the striking power of the militant.

But the Kashmiri component of the militancy is much smaller now than it used to be in the earlier part of the 90s, and that has relieved the pressure on the civil servant and the administration generally, who are closely affected by the mood of the people around them. There are also very credible reports that the youth in the Kargil area gave good logistical support in the wart against the invaders. The cumulative effect of these factors is that until darkness – and very cold evenings – descend on Srinagar the town sports a look of much greater normalcy than one had expected to see. Army elements are much less in evidence in the street than they used to be, and are able to concentrate more on areas closer to the border.

The Economy and Development

Important through they are for every state, the issues of the economy and development are particularly important for J & K. They affect the security of the state as well as a crucial plank of the state's relations with the Union. It is generally agreed that the reason why terrorist outfits based in Pakistan are able to find recruits in J & K is as much economic as its ideological. Unemployed youth, many of them with university education, are attracted by the financial inducements offered by Pakistan despite the risks involved in the activities they are then required to embrace, and in turn they become more motivated recruiting agents themselves.

Lack of other opportunities for jobs also makes them ready victims of the corrupt ways in which J&K's own politicians sell jobs to them, at extortionist prices, out of quotas of jobs which are allotted to them by the government for political patronage. The damage this directly does to the effectiveness of the administration is obvious enough. But equally serious is the indirect damage. For every one person who gets a job ten are disappointed, and anger against the whole political and governmental system grows exponentially. As some jobs are sold the state's security forces also, the state's security system is also imperiled.

Suspicion about corruption in the state's administration is also disrupting the equally essential task of economic development, and here too the damage is both direct and indirect. Directly there is leakage and wastage of money, and such developmental works as are undertaken are undermined. But more seriously, willingness to invest in the state, scarred off as it is by the fear of insecurity, is deterred by the fear of becoming infructuous. Since most of the investment comes from the Government of India, the latter also holds back. This is misunderstood as political blackmail of "Kashmir" by "India", is misrepresented as such to the people of the state, anger grows, security and development recede, the feeling of helplessness in the administration grows.

The Administration and Society

The stock of competence in the administration is considerable, and exceptional at some of the higher levels, both in the political and developmental fields. At the lower levels, its presence at its posts is also said to have improved because, for the reasons mentioned earlier, the pressures of the militancy upon it are said to have abated.

Among the worst sufferers of this overall impasse is the social fabric of the state, which was one of its most endearing distinctions at one time, producing such a mix of Hindu and Muslim traditions that it became a culture which was the best known bridge across the communal divide which has plagued India for centuries. One kind of intolerance is now breeding another kind across the divide. This has driven out the Kashmiri pandits from their homes, adding one more chapter to the chronical of their exoduses from the state. With them have gone some of the ablest and most productive elements in the population, and as the ablest among these strike root elsewhere only the least enterprising remain. Hopes of the revival of that old demography, and therefore of that old culture, are receding according one of the more perceptive and able Kashmiri administrators that one met. And he was among the more optimistic about what could or should be done.

PART-II
THE MOVING PICTURE

Introduction

The Pace of the Change

Unlike Part I which has three large overviews covering scenes close to home and farther apart, but all three taken from static points of time, Part II has over a dozen snapshots of more specific aspects taken in relatively quick succession and very recently. Between them they convey some of the movement which has taken place in the affairs of India, Pakistan, and the state of Jammu and Kashmir. They also explain the many new interactions between the three which have resulted from recent changes. The fact that the latest article urges a return to the Lahore process and so does one of the earliest shows, correctly, that the pace is slow. But it also shows how important the "process" has become. The description of a reaction between some Indians and Pakistanis in Geneva, depicted in the article "Return to Lahore But Carefully" also indicates the quality of a change.

In between lie a series of quick steps which show that the pace, particularly in Jammu and Kashmir, has not been too slow either. Comparison with the many years of stalemate from the late 1980s to the late 1990s confirms this view. The most interesting part of this period has been in the middle, when the scene in Kashmir changed from "Hope and Despair" to a "A Pregnant Pause" to "A Creditable Election"; and changed in Pakistan, over a slightly longer period, from games with "Hurriyat in a Changing Role" to "Soul Searching in Pakistan". To this period also belongs the fascinating change which came about in the ranks of the violently militant who began to reassess themselves as a result of a growing cleavage between those who saw themselves as the storm troopers of Pakistan and those who were focussed on the long term interests of Kashmir.

The most telling sign of the change has been the nature of the election which took place in Kashmir in the autumn of 2002, telling because of the reasons and the way it came about, and because of its outcome. It has created a unique government in Kashmir, the like of which has not existed before, and its legitimacy and quality has received higher praise than of any election in the state since the mid-1980s.

1

"Return To Lahore, But Carefully"

Mid, 2003

Prime Minister Vajpayee has been publicly raining gestures of peace on Pakistan in recent weeks. In the meantime a group of Indians and Pakistanis, veterans of peace making exercises on official and non-official tracks, have been conferring privately on how best some progress may be made.

Such efforts are not new. The sub-continent is crowded with such tracks, and traffic on many of them has been getting heavier of late. What is new however is the speed with which a broad consensus, even if imprecise as yet, has emerged on one track at least on what should be attempted when and what should be left over till better times. The consensus is neither limited to singing the virtues of peace nor pretends to prescribe comprehensive agreements, here and now. But it does mark a stage, cautiously but concretely, neither ignoring the probability that much bigger hurdles may lie farther ahead nor remaining stuck in the grooves of past disagreements.

This track, like others, has been provided by "facilitators". But it bears no mark of the "pressures" which imaginative people in both India and Pakistan see emerging from every third country plane that lands in either. Such progress as has now been made on this track has mainly resulted from one change : that instead of trying to rubbish agreements made in the past or failing to learn from past mistakes, a conscious effort has been made to see what can be built, and how, upon earlier gains. This change has also helped everyone to see once again that the best gains were made when the effort was most clearly bilateral and indigenous, without third party interests playing collateral games.

The consensus in question emerged over just two meetings, together lasting less than one week, one in early November last year and the next in mid-May this year, both in Geneva, both under the auspices of the Pugwash Workshops On South Asian Security. Under the protocol of the Workshops, what is said by whom may not be cited or quoted without the permission of the concerned participant. But enough has been permitted by some participants or made public by Pugwash itself on its own website to show the extent of the consensus.

As was narrated on this page soon after the first meeting, in November last year, a prominent participant from Pakistan, General Assad Durrani, former head of the all-powerful ISI, enlivened the proceedings there by remarking that the three documents resulting from the Lahore summit between Prime Ministers Nawaz Sharrif and Vajpayee had created an "an opportunity" but unfortunately it was "squandered". This was also the view of the Indian side of the summit when it saw that General Musharraf, who had banished Sharrif from Pakistan after staging a military coup against him, was also busy burying the summit and the "opportunity" created by it.

Therefore General Durrani's constructive description of the documents prompted an Indian participant in the November meeting to suggest that Pugwash should invite General Durrani to constitute a small group of Indian and Pakistani participants to see how best the "opportunity" may be revived, if necessary by revising and updating the documents too. No one opposed the suggestion, but it got shelved when the discussion took an acrimonious turn later on the unrelated issue of why the Agra summit had failed.

However, when Pugwash began to draw up the agenda for the meeting held in mid-May this year, an Indian invitee suggested that the programme should include a revisit to "the Lahore process." The suggestion prospered, and when the re-visit began General Durrani widened the "opportunity" by saying that even better than the Lahore documents was an agreement signed by the Foreign Secretaries of the two countries in 1997. The implications of what he said are as interesting as the reasons he gave for saying it, and the reasons as well as the implications would be widely acceptable in India.

He said the 1997 agreement covered a broad and yet integrated agenda, and while it was inevitable that progress on some issues would be slower than on others there would be a "synergy" between them, the speed of progress on some prodding the slower coaches as well. Few in India would disagree with this reason. Fewer still with the first implication, that since the 1997 agreement was a purely bilateral effort, the merit seen in it by the General gives greater depth to the chronology of successful bilateralism, extending it back into times when the norm was third party intervention.

Second, it showed Pakistan was no longer rigid on a stand which Indian interlocutors had found to be frustrating for years, that nothing can be discussed until the Kashmir issue is solved. Much else can be discussed, he implied, so long as Kashmir also is. Kashmir was of course a "core issue", but he argued in his quietly irrepressible way that you cannot reach the core of anything without dealing with the crust. Third, Pakistan has at last responded to the advice its closest friend, China, had given to it way back in the mid-90s, that a difficult issue was sometimes made more amenable if easier issues were solved in the meantime.

Fourth, since the "Lahore documents" signed by Prime Ministers Sharrif and Vajpayee are basically a re-make of the 1997 agreement, they show that summits are more at lower levels. In other words, a rush to the summit, as at Agra is better avoided than attempted. And finally the fifth, that with skilful preparation at appropriate levels, even touchy issues can be smoothly taken on board at summits, as the nuclear ambitions or fears of the two countries were in Lahore. The nuclear issue was not even mentioned in the 1997 agreement because neither country had carried out nuclear explosions till then. By 1999 it had mushroomed into the hottest issue between the two countries, next only to Kashmir. And yet it was not only taken up at Lahore but, as can be seen in the texts crafted by experts on the two sides, some intricate and far reaching approaches were adopted.

There is no implication here, none at all, that part time peacemakers finally won the day last mid-May in Geneva, point, set, and match. No, the game has not even begun as yet, and India still faces a cruel enigma, whether or not you may call India's position on it a "precondition" for talking to Pakistan. The enigma is in two parts.

First, wherever the Indo-Pakistan border might come to be in Jammu and Kashmir as the result of a settlement, whether along the present or a modified Line of Control, or along the border as it existed at the time of the creation of Pakistan,. given the present ethnic, religious, political and geographical terrain of the western strip of the state, it will always be vulnerable to the kind of violence jehadi bands can work up in their lairs on the Pakistan side unless Pakistan decides to nip them in the bud. Second, however large the fund of goodwill at the negotiating table, either the Indian or the Pakistani hand will freeze in the act of signing if cries of the victims of clashes break in through the window. To what avail will all the negotiating be then ?

A very senior Pakistani participant gave a partial answer to that, and an Indian counterpart gave a response. The former said let a stable peace first settle into normalcy before trying to find new frontiers, and in the meantime take every step with the utmost care. The latter said it would be enough for the day if broad principles were settled first and details left for better times to fill in. In the general spirit of consensus which existed at the meeting, no one disagreed with either.

2

Soul Searching in Pakistan

Early, 2003

The politics of the situation is important. But the irony of it fascinating, and so comes first. The truth behind it cannot be hidden by Musharraf's recent ranting at the NAM summit in Kuala Lumpur.

When Soviet troops marched into Afghanistan some twenty-five years ago, Mrs Indira Gandhi rushed her Foreign Minister, then Mr Narasimha Rao, to Pakistan to assure President General Zia that India would not take any advantage of this development at the expense of Pakistan. Mr Rao went further. At a public meeting which the Indian Counsel-General in Karachi managed to arrange for him, he made the Indian assurance public, and then added the proposal that India and Pakistan should put their heads together to see how they could jointly handle the event.

Pakistan asked that as proof of its goodwill India should cut its forces on the Indo-Pak border by half. India suspected that Zia wanted Indian troops on the border to be reduced because he wanted to free his forces for use against the Russians in Afghanistan. And so Zia's proposal, Mr Rao's mission and Mrs Gandhi's initiative all ended in smoke.

But a few years later India's suspicion about Zia's

motives gained colour because, with massive military assistance pouring into Afghanistan for use by the Taliban against Russian forces, Zia began to dream of using Afghanistan as a stepping stone for building an Islamic empire stretching from the river Ravi in the south and east, Iran in the west, the Russian river Volga in the north, and incorporating Kashmir and all the Central Asian republics of what was then the Soviet Union south of the Volga. The dream hardened as Soviet troops retreated in the face of the Taliban forces, which were now increasingly commanded by Pakistan expertise, armed by America, and egged on by the Islamic alliance, the IOC.

But before the dream could take further shape, a nightmare followed : Pakistan's domestic polity, undermined by the backwash of the radical Talibanisation which had taken over Afghanistan, went into a spin, all the more so after the mysterious assassination of Zia himself. This began to worry the conservative Islamic regimes of Pakistan's neighbours, as well as communist China because some Chinese areas adjacent to Pakistan are populated by disaffected Muslims.

Worse followed after the Russian withdrawal from Afghanistan and the fall of the Soviet Union. The infectious zeal of the Taliban gave birth to the even more dangerous epidemic of the Al Qaida. Much of the world began to huddle together against it. America took control of all of Zia's imagined empire from Kabul to the Russian border. Putin consolidated Russia within its reduced borders. America became busy with its games elsewhere in the Middle East. Extremist Islamists, sworn enemies of Musharraf's pro-American tilt and suspected by China, took control of the two western provinces of Pakistan, adjacent to Afghanistan, and also became a force in the central government of Pakistan. All the schemes Islamabad tried against Kashmir were defeated by India, first militarily in Kargil and then politically in the Kashmir valley. Hence the political somersault in the past few weeks by General Musharraf, the first military dictator of Pakistan since General Zia.

Between them the two Generals had committed the political – and in one case the physical — assassination of all the four democratically elected civilian prime ministers that the present day Pakistan had known : Zulfikar Ali Bhutto, Junejo, Benazir Bhutto, and Nawaz Sharrif. This reduced Pakistan politics to a shambles at the same time as it faced its worst foreign policy crisis, with America turning to its own games in the Middle East, China becoming colder, the Islamic neighbours more cautious, and India, enraged by jehadi terrorism, fully mobilised on its entire border with Pakistan. When his policies began to backfire one after the another at home and abroad, Musharraf rushed to Moscow three weeks ago and proclaimed Putin to be the best man for pulling the chestnuts out of the fire for him. All that remains for Musharraf to do to re-run the Narasimha Rao reel in reverse is to say India and Pakistan should put their heads together for jointly facing the crisis that looms as American troops prepare to March into Iraq.

But the reversal in Pakistan is best illustrated by some outstanding soul searching in the Pakistan press. Writing in the boldest newspaper in the country, *The Friday Times,* which he now edits, the well known commentator Najam Sethi says Musharraf is right in describing his Moscow visit as "historic" but he wryly adds it has been "fifty years overdue" because, as he explains, "If after independence we had been more 'neutral' like India we might have escaped the crippling dependence on the United States, (might have) prohibited the rise of the military as the sole determinant of our 'national security' ... made peace rather than war ... with our neighbour to the east" and avoided "the proxy war with Moscow in the 1980s" in Afghanistan into which, he says, Pakistan was "prodded by the United States".

Recalling that USA was "packing its bags in Pakistan" in 1987, Sethi argues "that would have been a good time" to start "'patching up' not just with the new Moscow but also with the old New Delhi... But a band of military adventurers had other ideas. They wanted to conquer Afghanistan, dominate Central Asia, and carve a green crescent from Turkey to Chechenya". He welcomes the termination of Zia's Afghan policy by Musharraf but adds Pakistan should also have started "thinking of how to wrap up our pro-active Kashmir policy before it started undermining dividends reaped from abandoning the Afghan policy. He recommends a Kashmir settlement "without redrawing boundaries" (a settlement along the Line of Control ?) but also cautions Pakistan against "the fiery insistence of the Kashmir jehadies that they are readying to carry the war from Srinagar to New Delhi".

A former editor of the same paper, Khaled Ahmad, analysing Musharraf's approach to normalising relations with India, says "Normalisation with an economically and militarily superior India has been made conditional by Pakistan to the undoing of the status quo while its internal weakness and international isolation undermines its foreign policy stance. Much of its internal weakness has stemmed from its deniable use of mercenary warriors in its 'low-intensity conflict' with India over the status quo. While normalisation has been made realistic by its possession of a nuclear deterrent vis-à-vis India, Pakistan's insistence on using it to force a change in the status quo has isolated it internationally. The measure of this isolation was revealed recently by General Musharraf when he disclosed that the Islamic world was no longer willing to include Pakistan's view of the Kashmir dispute in the OIC agenda. There was even an attempt by the Islamic states to allow India to join the OIC. As civil society struggles for survival in the ideological state of Pakistan, much of the decision-making in it is triggered, not by strategic thinking, but by a process of obsolescence in its foreign policy."

The course of Indo-Pakistan history over the past 30 years or more is too thickly littered with the debris of peace efforts for anyone to be very optimistic about the success of Musharraf's expectation that his journey to Moscow will do what so many earlier efforts by so many others were not able to do. But it remains a significant event that for the first time ever since the Tashkent conference in Moscow in 1965, Moscow has lent itself to a triangular effort to make peace between India and Pakistan, and it is still more significant that the effort to involve Moscow has been initiated this time by Pakistan.

The conference in 1965 was brought about by the Soviet leadership of the day, and possibly also with some suggestions by Washington, both the superpowers being prodded by the apprehension that Indo-Pakistan tensions might again be used by China, as they were in 1962, when China was able to take a slice of Pakistan-occupied Kashmir territory from Pakistan, and as they were used again in 1971 when Pakistan began a long term affair with China as a hedge against India and, to some extent, against America. The Simla meeting, between Mrs Indira Gandhi and Z.A. Bhutto, the series of meetings between Rajiv Gandhi and Benazir Bhutto, then between the Indian Prime Minister, I.K. Gujral and the Pakistan Prime Minister Nawaz Sharrif, and both of the two meetings between Musharraf and Vajpayee resulted only from efforts begun in these two countries though others also made encouraging noises from the sidelines. But it is for the first time that a triangular attempt has been initiated by Pakistan though it is possible that a triangular outcome at some future date was assumed to be a condition by both

Musharraf and Putin when they agreed to meet. This is one reason for some optimism.

A second reason is that, as the commentaries in the Pakistan press make so amply clear, there is a much greater understanding in Pakistan now than there has ever been in the past that Pakistan can no longer afford the war games it has played with India for half a century. War was never an option chosen by India. Pakistan has never chosen any other option. The reason may have only been that since Kashmir was already a part of India there was no reason for India to go to war for getting it, whereas Pakistan knew that war was the only way for it, however the ruinous the consequences might be for it. But whatever the reasons the fact remains that war for Kashmir was always thrust upon India, never initiated or sought by it. Now Pakistan realises that even war will not do.

A third reason : It is strange but true that faster than any other person one can think of, Putin has become a trusted figure in many situations of dispute between countries, although hardly anyone outside Russia and not many inside it knew much about him when he became the President of Russia. There is something about his personal chemistry which is quite unique. He has a firm grasp of essentials, and he puts them firmly on the table, thus forestalling later misunderstandings. He displayed these qualities even in his somewhat brief interaction with Musharraf last month. He made it clear to Musharraf that no effort to reach agreements would be worth making unless there was full assurance than the agreements reached would be fully observed. And he made it known to India that he had made this clear to Musharraf. Therefore, future talks between India and Pakistan, as he told both countries, must begin on the basis of the Simla and Lahore agreements, even if only to discuss whether they needed to be updated or altered, and that too could only be done by agreement.

And of course above all other reasons for some optimism there is the reason that India and Pakistan have an even greater need now than ever before to resolve their differences because of the war clouds hanging over the Middle East, the most significant Muslim majority area in the world which is likely to see the war as a clash between faiths. Pakistan's population is almost entirely Muslim. India has the second largest Muslim population in the world. Both will be affected in complex ways by the impending war, and neither will be fully able to deal with the complexities to its full ability without fully understanding the large Muslim block just across the border.

3

Tragedy and Response

Early, 2003

Like a nut caught in a cracker, the plight of the Kashmiri Pandits of Jammu and Kashmir is a concentrated tragedy caught within the larger tragedy of the state as a whole. One of the most talented members of the larger Hindu family and of the still larger Indian family, this community has contributed to India its first and most famous Prime Minister, Pandit Nehru; a later successor to that office, Indira Gandhi; the most famous patriarch of the freedom movement, Pandit Motilal Nehru; and many notable administrators, diplomats, and luminaries of the legal and judicial professions. Kashmiri Pandits were also the pillars of the state's administration under Dogra rule. But above all, along with their Muslim neighbours the Kashmiri Pandits produced Kashmir's greatest gift to India, "Kashmiriyat", that particularly fragrant mix of the best in Hindu and Muslim customs, beliefs, manners and rituals which so attracted Gandhi when he was searching for the roots of secularism. As a result a living closeness developed between Hindus and Muslims in Kashmir for which there are few parallels.

Yet, ever since India became independent the Kashmiri Pandits, like their fountainhead, the valley of Srinagar, have suffered a series of calamities, beginning with what happened to them in 1947 when fanatics invaded Kashmir from Pakistan and burnt and looted Kashmiris in the name of Islam. Worse was to follow, as the ranks of the invaders were swelled by the Pakistan army, and by terrorists and jehadies. What happened on March 25 in the village of Nadimarg in Pulwana is only a further outburst of the same process. More than a score of Pandits were killed in their homes by terrorists, with local Muslims taking part in the carnage, including members of the local police.

It has happened to others also, as for example has happened on a much larger scale to Indian Muslims as a whole, that those who were rulers once become the subjects later of those over whom they had ruled. The inversion excites the anger of each side against the real or imagined wrongs done to it by the other side. The process has rubbed its way into Kashmir as well, driven by those interested parties which have kept the "Kashmir issue" on the boil with cooked up excuses.

Pakistan argues that because India had been partitioned on the basis of religion and Kashmir had a Muslim majority, therefore the state should have acceded to India. The argument is false because the partition plan, drawn up and implemented by Britain, had nothing to do with the religion of its people as the basis on which a territory might choose between joining India or Pakistan. The partition scheme makes not a mention of it. Equally false is Pakistan's argument that India must fulfill a commitment it made under a UN resolution of the late 1940s that it would hold a plebiscite in the state to decide its future. The Indian commitment was subject to prior fulfillment of three commitments by Pakistan. These have not been fulfilled by Pakistan even to this day, and in the meantime the UN itself came to the conclusion, in 1957, that on account of their non-fulfillment for ten long years it was no longer practicable to carry out the resolution.

Like its many predecessors the latest massacre might not be a "strategic setback" as it has been called by some in the context of Pakistan's threat to India. But such a large human tragedy cannot but cause second thoughts in the state and central government's plans about the future safety of Kashmiri Pandits, of whom thousands have been living in pitiable conditions for years outside Kashmir. When the Deputy Prime Minister, Mr Advani, went to Nadimarg he was roughly mobbed by those demanding migration to safety. His response underlines the government's dilemma. He could not refuse such a natural demand by them, but he urged them to consider that such ethnic cleansing of Kashmir was just what the enemy wanted.

He was right. But tragedies of this magnitude can stir public demands which may be shortsighted but cannot always be resisted, as the government found in the wake of the highjacking of an IAC plane a couple of years ago. Therefore it is necessary that clarity be reached very soon on the question whether the problem of the safety of Kashmiri Pandits is a part of the problem of the security of the state as a whole or is it a specific which needs to be treated separately. The two approaches are different and lead to different remedies. Either may be as good or bad as the other but vacillation between the two can make both of them ineffective.

There have been very welcome reports that the Muslims of Nadimarg have been assuring their Pandit neighbours that they will be safe in future. They have also been pleading with them not to emigrate. There are some even more welcome reports that some of the surviving Pandits have agreed to give these promises a chance. That would be the best remedy. Emigration from anywhere can hurt, but leaving Kashmir can be cruel; and success in Nadimarg can catch on. Besides, success there can prove again that no safety can be stronger for two neighbours than trust between them. But with things being what they are, left to themselves the promises may prove to be fragile against unpredictable winds. Such as another gust of communal passion, or the avarice of a neighbour who hopes to inherit the assets of an emigree, or a policeman who is a disguised infiltrator.

Therefore the joint policy of the governments in Srinagar and New Delhi, to encourage the Pandits to return to their homes, is too precious - and too valuable — to be left to chance. It needs several reinforcements. First, the state government's very wise "healing touch" should have no chinks which infiltrators may use. Second, safety of specific localities must form part of and not run counter to the overall safety of the state, because that is where the mother of all chinks may lie, providing entry points for the infiltrator. Third, the intended destinations of the returning migrants must be first made secure, whether by the selective location of police posts or selective resettlement of retiring security personnel in mixed neighbourhoods. Fourth, the destinations themselves must be confined for the time being to belts of relatively greater security. Fifth, grief over the deaths of innocent people must not become a gift for the enemy in psychological warfare, because it is that which makes it a "strategic setback". Finally it must be made plainer than it might be yet that crimes like the Nadimarg massacre carry a price which has to be paid one day.

All this might read like a well worn sermon. But it is not. It is a simple but long ignored truth. Virtually the same thing happened a few years ago in another village. More than 20 Pandits were killed and many more driven out by fear of actual violence. The same promises were made by similar neighbours. But no lessons were learnt, and Nadimarg followed.

4

A Pregnant Pause

Early, 2002

As I write these lines, South Asia is passing through what I can only describe as " a pregnant pause." The reason : Important events are impending. It is not known what they will be or when they will occur. But they will change things, whether for better or for worse. Between Pakistan and India in the first place, but at some remove wider afield also.

General Musharraf has publicly promised he will announce some in the next few days. Prominent American politicians who called on him on January 8 have heightened expectations. They think he is planning a breakthrough initiative. They might or might not be right. Sometimes a person who does not know the full picture is carried away by a small detail. Itinerant politicians often fall into that trap, and Americans in particular are prone to believe about Pakistan what they wish to believe. But the situation is indeed fraught with possibilities. When the armies of two old enemies are on high alert and standing face to face, a standstill cannot last long. Either things will ease and a stand down will follow. Or something else will.

A source of comfort is that a flash point seems a little less imminent now than it did till it recently. It receded in three stages but all within less than a month. On December

13 terrorists carried out their most daring attack on India so far : on Parliament House in New Delhi. This aroused angry resolution in India, more intense than seen even during regular wars between the two countries. Other countries sat up to take notice of the Indian mood, and in the second stage they put pressure upon Pakistan to back down. Pakistan began to do so in the third stage, and India also withdrew its fist to its back. But the logic of the situation continues to be grim.

General Musharraf has put some curbs on some terrorist organisations in his country, and has promised some more in the next few days. He has also promised a long haul effort to make more space for moderate Islam, which the fundamentalists have been pushing into a corner. India has welcomed these steps, officially and publicly, and has agreed to wait to see more of them. But India also finds them to be insufficient, unconvincing, and, what is more serious, unrelated to India's highest concerns.

India has noted, with regret, that most of the measures announced or promised by President Musharraf are related to organisations to which the West objects, not to those which have made India their target. As much as other countries, India would also be happier with a Pakistan which has the "more balanced society" promised by Musharraf in his talks with the British PM, Tony Blair. But what India wants more urgently is a Pakistan which shows it has learnt that it cannot get through terrorism what it could not get by attacking India with its regular armed forces.

With the major western powers backing it, India insists that any future terrorists attack against it must evoke as resolute a response as America gave to the bombing of the World Trade Centre, whether the attack be made in the name of *jehad* or anything else for ending Indian rule in Kashmir. In addressing South Asian leaders at the summit meeting of SAARC a few days ago in Kathmandu General Musharraf still insisted that a distinction be made between aiding terrorists and aiding "freedom fighters."

His view was rejected by SAARC, the South Asian Association for Regional Cooperation, and he went along with the joint declaration by the Association which is comprehensively against all forms of terrorism in support of any political cause or objectives. But his actions in Pakistan continue to be guided by that distinction. This has made things easy for those terrorist organisations which are based in Pakistan but practice their murderous art in Kashmir. When their existing name is banned but not their aims or methods, they simply reappear under another name and pick up from where they had temporarily left off.

It has been pleaded on his behalf by some western apologists that since his predecessors had fed militancy against Kashmir for years he cannot switch it off overnight. Colour is lent to this view by what General Hamid Gul has just said. As the intelligence boss at Pakistan's army headquarters for many years he had nurtured *jehadi* organisation and continues to champion their cause in his retirement. From that position he warned Musharraf in a BBC broadcast on January 7 that while he could get away with suppressing terrorists who operated within Pakistan, he would be in trouble if he impeded their activities in Kashmir. But India's concern is not with what will get Musharraf into trouble or keep him out of it. India wants to see him do what will keep Pakistani terrorists out of India. If he does not do it India will have to do it for him. That will determine how the present pause will end.

But what rankles India is the distinction Pakistan makes between them and the Taliban in Afghanistan. Pakistan was the master mind behind the Taliban in

Afghanistan. They were as much its off-spring as are the terrorists who operate against India. The Pakistan army, more particularly its intelligence wing, and all the more so General Hamid Gul himself, were the handlers of both the Taliban and the anti-India terrorists. Yet they were able to cut themselves off fast enough from the Taliban when American bombers gave them incentives enough to do so. So Pakistan's difficulty is not that it cannot abandon very quickly those whom it had nursed for long. Its difficulty, or rather India's, is that Pakistan has not yet been given incentives enough to abandon the terrorists as well.

That means something which is doable for Pakistan and acceptable for India has yet to emerge. In the meantime, fire continues to smoulder on the Indo-Pakistan border. If it does not emerge in the steps which General Musharraf is said to have promised, then it can only emerge out of such additional incentives that India can furnish. Therefore to much should not be read too soon into the current pause. It is pregnant, for sure. But with what?

5

A Creditable Election

·Early, 2002

Party managers and bosses will spend many days in ruminating over what the voter has done to their hopes and plans as a result of the state level elections which have just ended. But the voter has done his own job very well. He has asserted his preferences through the very legitimate process of free elections, and the poorer and more "backward" voter has done so even more than the better off. He has not allowed the frequency of elections to dampen his faith in the ballot box. He has neither yielded to intimidation nor to the temptation of divisive or extremist slogans.

As a result : Many a gun totting candidate has been defeated, though not all. Political parties have shown a broader outlook. The party system is now healthier because fewer votes have gone to splinter parties and more states now have a two or three front if not a two or three party polity. Most votes have been polled by moderate views. There is some evidence of a shift to bread and butter issues from religious shibboleths, and lack of performance has been punished, as it deserved to be. The election machinery has worked well, delivering results very quickly despite the vastness of numbers and distances in a state like UP. Electoral voting has been proved a success even in constituencies which had never seen these machines before.

Some problems continues : that a small shift in a party's share of the votes makes a disproportionate difference in its share of seats, thus making the legislature a less true reflection of the electorate. Similarly the way a legislature forms and changes governments promotes instability. But these are not faults of the voter or political parties. Much more to blame is the fact that we are sticking to voting systems which served us well for a time but now need a change, both in the way the country elects its legislature and the way the legislatures form or change governments. Parliament must consider some changes in both. But as elections held under the given systems, the round which has just ended has been more creditable than many earlier ones. Unfortunately they have also cast an ominous shadow, to which I will come later. But first the brighter spots.

The best among them is that the bitter gulf which had persisted for more than a quarter century between the Sikhs and the Congress appears to have ended. The gulf had been opening since the early 1980s but widened dangerously with the attack on the Golden Temple and the assassinations of Mrs Indira Gandhi and Sant Longowal. An earlier success of the Congress in winning a substantial share of Sikh votes was undone by the assassination of the Congress Chief Minister, Mr Beant Singh, because the after shocks of operation Blue Star were continuing at that time. Who was primarily responsible for those tragedies, the Sikh Congress leaders who sowed the seeds of Sikh militancy in the early 1980s or those militants who converted it into an armed mutiny against the country can be debated for another quarter century. But its ghosts began to be laid by a very welcome political partnership during much of the past decade between the BJP, a party strong among the Hindus of Punjab, and the Shromani Akali Dal, which was even stronger among the Sikhs. It is not certain how well that partnership will continue to thrive at the centre after its defeat in Punjab. But for the present it now exists on both sides of the new Punjab legislature, on the Opposition benches as an open coalition between the Akali Dal and BJP, and on the Treasury Benches as an internal coalition within the victorious Congress, which has resumed the role it had played for thirty years after independence as a party representing both Hindus and Sikhs, and now under the robustly secular, moderate, and modernist leadership of Mr Amrindar Singh. Its high share of the total vote in this election shows it has polled well among both communities. If the message received by Akali leaders is that reputation for corruption invites retribution then this is good for everyone, whether the reputation was justified or not.

It is also a welcome feature of the process that the polity is now a lot more bi-polar than in earlier elections, and the splinter groups are much less in evidence than they were in some of the earlier elections. There is an unfortunate imbalance between the share of seats and of votes between the two sides. But that only reinforces the case for a reconsideration of the first past the post electoral system.

In a similar way if not to the same extent, societal gulfs have been narrowed a little in Uttar Pradesh because of the nature of the choices made by some of the political parties, and by the campaigns accordingly run by them. The best example of that, but not the only one, is the Bahujan Samaj Party. In earlier elections it used to raise its Dalit appeal to the highest pitch, presumably in a hyper effort to mobilise them as its base, and it has been very successful in this effort. It is also the main reason why it has been able to perform better than either of the two other main contestants, the BJP alliance and the Samajwadi Party. But having got what it could out of its exclusivist campaigns earlier, it has this time tried to reach out to upper castes more boldly than it had ever done before, and this is bound to soften its earlier and more aggressive image and might also widen its options at the state level and perhaps also in New Delhi.

In the meantime the same clearing up of the clutter has happened in UP as in Punjab, the same softening of the lines dividing parties, and the same moving away from yesterday's slogans. Most of the vote has gone to the three main contenders and very little to splinters and "rebel candidates" fighting as "independants." Mulayam Singh has by and large stuck to his Muslim and Yadav platform, perhaps believing it to be such a winning ticket that he would rather not tamper with it. How this might affect his post-election manoeuverability is a riddle which will unfold only with time but some adjustments might be forced upon him by two changes in the base of his support. First, in an effort to defeat BJP candidates, some among his Muslim supporters are reported to have shifted towards whichever party appeared to them to be a better bet in this game; and second, a section of the Kurmi vote, a caste next lower to Mulayam Singh's most loyal supporters, the Yadavs, has branched out into a party of its own and has thus weakened him in several constituencies. These developments might modify the profile and prospects of his Samajwadi Party and in the meantime demonstrate to him and others that certain games do not pay because others can play them too.

But a change more pregnant with possibilities has been made by his main opponent, the BJP. It has been clear for some time that Prime Minister Vajpayee's main strategy in dealing with the Masjid-Mandir controversy has been to cool the issue even if he cannot resolve it through negotiations, so that there may be less fanatical opposition, whether by the Muslims or Sadhus, to whatever decision might come out of the Supreme Court, which is now the only route left for some decision. For this reason it was of the utmost importance for him that his own party at least should not add fuel to this fire even if it meant some loss of enthusiasm among the party's cadres.

This message went home, though not well in time. As soon as he took charge as Chief Minister Mr Rajnath Singh began to distance himself, his party and his government from the Ram Temple platform of some of the more vociferous members of the Sangh Parivar. He spoke much more about issues of development than of communal divides, much more than any BJP leader of that standing had done in U.P. This had a corresponding effect on the other side, and therefore not much was heard about the Babri Masjid either. In no election since the mid-90s has less been heard about the temple-masjid controversy, nor have more voters said so candidly and on camera that their daily problems matter more to them and demands for this or that place of worship are only the pastime of politicians.

Closely related is the fact that though many circumstances had converged to arouse communal sentiments they caused much less disturbance than might have been expected. There was for example the vastly accentuated awareness of terrorism by organisations openly claiming to be or accused of being Islamic jehadies, there were vivid reports about their brutalities on behalf of what they called their Islam, there was still smouldering anger about their attack on Parliament House in New Delhi, suspicion about terrorists defeated in Afghanistan infiltrating into India, evidence of Pakistan aiding the process, the greatly heightened tension and military preparedness on both sides of the Indo-Pakistan border. But in all parts of Uttar Pradesh they disturbed the electoral process much less than feared and much less than in some elections held in less heated time.

But before closing this comment one must not fail to say more about the "ominous shadow" to which reference was made earlier. Its effects could be insidious even if its manifestations were inconspicuous. It had been reported before the elections, rumoured even more widely, and confirmed by some of the election results, that Muslim voters had been quietly directed by their leaders or had decided spontaneously to focus on defeating BJP candidates no matter who they had to support for ensuring that. In the event such voting played a part in the electoral humbling of BJP. This can have three consequences, each worse than the others.

First, it can discourage other BJP leaders from following in the footsteps of Rajnath Singh, and that can squash the beginning he made towards secularising his party's electoral politics. Second, it can lend respectability to a communalist response from the other side. Third, it can widen the gulf between political activists on both sides. The mixture can be inflammatory.

6

13.12 After Six Months

Mid, 2002

The world owes thanks to all persons, organisations, countries, which have persuaded India and Pakistan to start pulling back as these lines are written. But India still needs to be watchful. The content of its policy is firm and clear. But the context in which it has to be implemented is still foggy. This is because terrorism has links with the Pakistan army, as confirmed by the British Foreign Minister, Jack Straw in the House of Commons, and the continuing ambivalence shown towards this issue by the American Departments of State and Defence in the past few days.

President Musharraf said on May 30 that it would be Pakistan's "utmost endeavour to avoid conflict". On June 1 he said on CNN that a nuclear war with India could be ruled out. On June 6 he said he would never "initiate" war with India. Richard Armitage, of the American State Department, patted him on the back for saying all that and promised he would seek the same assurances from New Delhi. But what Musharraf said completely mispresents the situation, and the response by Armitage shows how willingness to be misled.

The question is not, and has never been for the past 35 years, whether Pakistan would initiate a war with India.

since 1965, and even more since 1971, it has been clear to Pakistan what "war" with India can mean. That also became clear to Musharraf himself when he misled his own Prime Minister, Nawaz Sharrif, into the Kargil adventure.

The real question is, and has always been since the terrorist attack on the Indian Parliament on December 13 last year, what should India do if, firstly, Musharraf is unable or unwilling to stop terrorist activities against India from territories controlled by Pakistan"; and secondly, should Pakistan's threat of a nuclear reaction deter India from doing all that it needs to do to stop such activities.

Since long before 13.12, India's policy quite clearly has been, first, to cooperate with any country which claims it can persuade or pressure Pakistan into stopping terrorism against India. Second, if Pakistan takes steps to control infiltration of terrorists across the Line of Control, India will respond with appropriate steps, as Prime Minister Vajpayee announced at Almaty on June 4. Third, if such efforts fail and Indian security is put at serious risk, then India must do all it needs to do end the risk, undeterred by threats of a nuclear response by Pakistan. Fourth, while protecting itself India must stick to its commitment not to be the first to use a nuclear weapon. Fifth, in the event of a nuclear response by Pakistan to India's conventional efforts, India must respond in kind, undeterred by possible international reactions.

In the past six months, India has added four further dimensions to this policy. First, India has taken several steps of a non-military nature to make it clear not only to Pakistan but to all interested countries that India will no longer keep turning the other cheek. Second, at the military level, it has mobilised its forces massively around Pakistan. Third, it has announced its willingness to scale down or reverse these measures if, but only if, Pakistan effectively curbs does its terrorism against India, hands over to India those twenty persons whose names India gave Pakistan a few months ago, or least hands those among them who are of Indian origin, are known to be residing in Pakistan, and are guilty of terrorism against India. Fourth, India has promised a suitably calibrated response, in good faith, to any signs that Pakistan is at least trying to curb jehadi attacks on India.

It is difficult to see where in all this President Musharraf saw the need to assure Armitage that Pakistan would not "initiate" war against India, or Armitage saw the need to promise Pakistan that he would get the same assurances from India. Nevertheless, when Armitage said Musharraf had promised to put a permanent end to infiltrations across LoC, Foreign Minister, Jaswant Singh publicly responded the next day and said that "if" the promise was "converted on the ground into action ... India will reciprocate in a manner that is befitting." The was "if" was to lose its critical place in the next two days as India undertook some de-escalation without saying what action had been seen on the ground.

India also took note of the claim Armitage brought from Pakistan that the infiltration had gone down, although America's own assessment until a few days earlier had been different. Collin Powell had said on May 31 that though Musharraf was saying infiltration would be ended " we can still see evidence that it is continuing". On June 1 he went further on BBC. He said "I have seen indications that instructions have been given" in Pakistan "to cease this kind of activity. I think it is too early to say that it has stopped. And when, and if, it does stop it must also stop permanently." And he added India must also be able to see it had stopped, but "we did not see the kind of cessation that we were expecting based on what President Musharraf said in his January 12 speech." America firmed this view further on June 7 when the spokesman of the State Department said Pakistan must end "infiltration across the LoC on a permanent basis. And when that becomes evident, we look to the Indians to reciprocate." However "the Indians" were more ready to reciprocate than that.

It is not known what evidence India had of that "kind of cessation", apart from assurances received through American sources, before New Delhi announced the first de-escalatory steps on June 10, while the official Indian position till as recently as June 8 was that implementation of the promises made by Pakistan "will be carefully assessed, whereafter ... India will respond appropriately and positively". It is not known what implementation was effected by Pakistan between the two dates. But one comments is in order. If India already had the information on which it based these steps, then it would have been more graceful and more conducive to better relations with Pakistan to announce them as India response to that information, and to announce them directly to Pakistan. As seen above, assurances brought by America are sometimes coloured by inappropriate perceptions.

India has not had much joy out of America on the other issue either, that of the list of persons wanted by India. For some months after 13.12, America kept conveying messages that it was working with Pakistan on that list. US Ambassador Blackwill's refrain in his comments in Delhi was " We are working on it." Pakistan's on the other hand was that there was no question of handing over any Pakistani citizens and they did not have any of the non-Pakistani's named on the list. The stalemate was completed by the Pakistan Foreign Minister, Abdul Sattar, on June 9 when he said before there could be any extradition there had to be an extradition treaty. Negotiating one can take as long as either party wishes to prolong the process.

But it is quite wrong to fault India's policy or its implementation on any of the three or four counts on which they have been criticised. Such shortcomings as there are in India's handling of this crisis lie in the wider domain of national capabilities and performance, whether in the societal, security or other domains, plus the consequences of a clash between India's interests and those of countries which have a greater capacity to protect their stakes in any situation, or have a short term geo-strategic advantage in a particular situation. These are not imbalances which a country's foreign or security policy can rectify on its own.

The question has been raised whether all the diplomatic traffic between India, Pakistan, and some of the major western countries in recent months hasn't derailed India's thirty year old stand that Kashmir is a purely bilateral issue, to be resolved between India and Pakistan alone and without the intervention of a third country or other mediators. This is not so. In the days when bilateralism became the cornerstone of India's policy on the Kashmir issue, terrorism was not the threat that it first became to India's security in the 1990s and has since become to the security of many countries. It would have been ridiculous for India not to join hands with countries which are equally interested in fighting the scourge. But in joining with them India has in no way either invited or allowed them to mediate in the issue of the future political status of the state of Jammu and Kashmir. Collin Powell affirmed this unambiguously on May 31.

If their participation in India's own fight against terrorism or India's participation in their fight further sanctifies the Line of Control in Jammu and Kashmir then this only further strengthens the stand India took jointly with Pakistan in signing the Simla Agreement, which forbids use of force or threat to use it to change the Line in any way. It is possible that with or without the support of some other countries Pakistan will misread this as mediation. But India will be well enough able to deal with that, if and when it needs to.

The Government of India and the Foreign Ministry in particular can be criticised, as they have been above, for being too readily responsive to gestures by Pakistan, whether genuine or not. But each of the responses India has made so far can be reversed at no great cost if Pakistan goes back on its assurances, whether given directly to India or through other countries. In fact less cost than before because during the past few weeks many countries have held Pakistan guilty of terrorism and duplicity. This had not been the case either before September 11 or December 12, and since then nothing has prevented India from taking any measures which, in its overall judgement would be in India's interests.

7

Living With His Lies

Mid, 2002

Someone, somewhere, for some reason, has – to put it straight—deceived the Indian people, and they should get an explanation soon.

A clever lawyer may yet quibble that no one has gone back in so many words, in quotes, on what he can be shown to have said earlier in quotes. That may be a fact. But the effect is different. The cause may well be the spin put upon words whether by the speaker or by the media; or by high level carriers of confidential messages. But the effect is that for weeks people were given to understand something which now turns out to be something else, according to what has been said in so many words and in quotes.

If words, as reported, mean anything, various American and British dignitaries who have been visiting India have been telling us for weeks that President Musharraf is changing his ways, not only about society and politics in Pakistan but also about terrorism against India by infiltrators from across the Line of Control in J&K. Some of them have also been assuring India that if we gave him more time he would stop the infiltration.

Since we do not have a watchman of our own senior enough to read Musharraf's mind, we have been reading his intention only through the perceptions brought us by the visitors. This culminated in the rare occurrence that on June 16 Home Minister Advani and Defence Minister Fernandez said in identical words, as reported, that "a perceptible change" had taken place "in Pakistan's attitude."

But just about the same day Prime Minister Vajpayee gave an interview to *Newsweek* which, as published a few days later, quoted him as saying " There has been no change in Pakistan's policy so far as cross-border terrorism is concerned." Mr Vajpayee was not going by perceptions brought by travelling salesmen eager to sell their ware. He was speaking from visible and verifiable events happening on the Indian side of LoC.

Therefore all three members of the Indian government need to tell the people how they came to be so inconsistent with each other, and ask their visitors how they reconcile their reading of Musharraf, as conveyed by them to India, to Musharraf's flat denial of any intention or commitment to stop infiltration or to shut down his training camps for terrorists.

True, there has been a flurry of reports that at the highest level America and Britain have ticked the General off, that he has re-affirmed the commitments he had earlier made to the visitors. But, first, these reports have come through the same filters as had the earlier reports of the "commitments" he made. Second, we have no word at the time of this writing about what exactly was said to him at these levels nor about what was his reply. Third, there is no public word yet about what exactly are the commitments he has re-affirmed Fourth, we do not know whether this time too they leave him free to quibble tomorrow.

Until India gets answers to these questions it cannot decide whether it can trust Musharraf's latest "commitments" as reported on June 25. What India does know is that *after* he had chucked his earlier commitments out of the window, the US State Department could still say, on June 24 " We have no reason to disbelieve him." How consistent is that with the spate of Musharraf's interviews to the contrary which have lately cluttered wires, screens, front pages in preceding days? Or how consistent with each other are America's own assessments of the man when Rumsfeld says Musharraf cannot stop all infiltration even if he wants to, Powell says he can, and the General himself says he never said he would ?

These inconsistencies ought to be rectified before people begin to doubt the candour or honesty of their own ministers or their ability to perceive things correctly or the bonafide of those whom Mr Vajpayee described in his excellently worded interview as "facilitators ... not mediators". If the inconsistencies persist they will sour the very welcome and growing similarity of views in India, America and Britain, which has just been confirmed again by the reactions of all three countries to Musharraf's latest volte face. Most Indians understand America's right to have and pursue its own priorities, which are different from India's, but they would not like America to mislead them. As for Musharraf, India has lived with Pakistan's lies for long enough to know how to live with his.

India has hitherto steered its policy very creditably through these rocks and shoals, as brought out in the present author's article entitled "13.12 After Six Months". And India continues to do so. Hence on the one hand India's refusal to stand down on the border until Pakistan creates the right conditions for that, and its readiness on the other hand to talk with Pakistan after that. No new initiative is likely from either side until after the elections, due in a couple of months. Pakistan will continue to try to disrupt them, and will not want to let down the disruptors by being seen to be making peace with India before the poll. India will not want to give them any room for their tactics. But India does need to start looking soon beyond the elections.

The army cannot remain on the alert indefinitely, and not only on the long and difficult border of Kashmir but also on the still longer and no easier border of Punjab, Rajasthan and Gujarat. It needs to develop an appropriate concept of border defence, match it with a suitable mix of manpower and technical means, and back up both with public opinion which understands what is at stake. Only then can India overcome three advantages – the third is most important – which Pakistan has in making war upon India through infiltration and disruption in the name of jehad. If India neutralises these, as it certainly can, it can reduce both communalism and militancy to pin pricks.

First, Pakistan's agents can find crevices in India's social mosaic, from where they spread the tentacles of fanaticism. India cannot retaliate in kind. Nor should it even if it could. But surely India's security requires that nothing should be done which makes the crevices grow wider, more fertile, more numerous. Therefore India cannot afford the wrong ways BJP is treating Kashmir, on the autonomy issue particularly, or is treating UP by choosing Katyar as its face in India's most populous state, which also has the highest number of Muslims. He may have been chosen because of his caste identity, but he also carries the hated smell of Bajrang Dal. The government must stay firmly on the secular plank, while cleansing it of the thick coat of prejudices which it has acquired. For the rest the loyalty of every Indian must be treated as leak proof except where evidence shows it is suspect.

Second, while Indian forces can only move in numbers which easily show up even under remote surveillance, Pakistan's agents can slip across borders undetected, carrying weapons which are easily hidden and used. They cannot be stopped by any method which is both fool proof and affordable. No defending army and para forces can be strung out along a couple of thousand miles in an unbroken chain of eye contact, ready to ask for the ID of anyone in sight. That would be as foolish and wasteful a security doctrine as a military doctrine that the enemy must never be allowed to capture even an inch of territory, which is a sure way of losing a mile.

India's aim is to throw back the enemy, not to capture territory for any reason except for plugging a hole in defences. Therefore, using a mix of manual and technical surveillance, India must build a monitoring chain on the border and in the air above it which can detect any sizeable move by Pakistan. It needs to position military force only behind that chain, but with sufficient numbers and lateral mobility to repel any sizeable incursion. A retaliatory force only needs to be still farther behind that.

In building an adequate detecting chain India should rely on its own technologies as far as possible. But it need not worry too much that those who supply such sensors as we may need will be able to use them for spying on our movements for the suppliers' own purposes. If the supplier were America for example it would be able to use any of its many other means for watching our units closely enough for its own needs. Would America leak the information to Pakistan ? It did leak some to Israel about a surprise move by Nasser into Gaza. But that depends on the balance of its relations with India and Pakistan, and India has been plying this diplomatic game well enough for our needs.

But it is the third of Pakistan's three advantages which is the most difficult and at the same time the most important to neutralise. However, if you neutralise it once you have ended it for ever. This advantage is that the Indian public, pushed by the media, over-reacts more often than not, and goes from panic at one extreme to an uncontrollable outburst at the other. This paralyses considered policy at both ends, because in a vigorous democracy policy cannot by-pass the public for long. This has convinced Pakistan that India is like a heap of tinder. You throw a matchstick, and it will burst into a conflagration. You do a Godhra through your agents and the whole of Gujarat will burn. You hijack an IAC plane and the wailing relatives of the passengers, wailing even louder on television than in life, will force the government to concede any demand.

This is what has made the Pakistani militant more potent. The one you cannot stop at the border will sneak into a street and shoot off a dozen in a crowd. The public will cry the government has betrayed strategic national security, and if the army does not react drastically an impatient opposition leader will demand that the Prime Minister must resign. Others will float signals of a nuclear war. Interested powers will step in with their own agenda and demand control over our nuclear button. Thus the death of a few people at the hands of a single gun man who slips in can harm our national security more seriously than the death of many dozens in bus accidents all over the place. But if the country refuses to be stampeded by the terrorist, the army will remain free to choose its own time and place for a suitable retaliation. It is the terrorist who will then have died in vain, because found and shot he will be the next day or the next, and the war of terrorism will fizzle out.

8

Aims, Gains, and Traps in Kashmir

Late, 2002

With our habit of running ourselves down, we took little time to declare that all the good that had been done by the courageous elections in Jammu and Kashmir had been undone by the jostling between the Congress and the People's Democratic Party of Mufti Mohammad Sayeed for the post of Chief Minister. Some distress over the squabbling was justified, but those who said this had defeated the aim of the elections or betrayed the bravery of the voter misunderstood what this election was about. Its aim was much higher than only to decide who should rule the state for the next few years. The aim was nothing less than to rehabilitate the whole electoral process.

The earliest elections in the state had not only introduced it to the ways of democracy. They had also vindicated the faith of the first Chief Minister, Sheikh Abdullah, in the secular future of the state and his economic vision. But the process soon became a prisoner of the political exigencies imposed upon the state by the perfidy of Pakistan and the cold war objectives of the United States. This cloud was lifted for a time in the late 1970s and the early 1980s, when democratic commitments re-asserted themselves both in the country and in the state, and in Kashmir it was lifted further when Farooq Abdullah, standing on a secular platform, battled successfully against so formidable an opponent as India's Prime Minister then, Mrs Indira Gandhi, whose platform had strong communal overtones in that campaign. This success, and the affront to her power which was implicit in it, was perhaps one of the reasons why she dismissed him and his government soon afterwards. But thereafter democracy began to be undermined again when the National Conference in Srinagar and successive governments in New Delhi, each pleading its own political compulsions, derailed democracy in the state. In the mid-1980s Farooq Abdullah first created and then destroyed the chance of recovery, and a weak leadership in Delhi could do little to prevent him.

Communalisation of electoral politics had always been a danger in the state, as it seemed at the time it raised a threatening head when the state began to prepare for the last election of the 1980s. An able and effective leader of the frankly communal party, Jamaat-I-Islami, Ghulam Mohammad Bhat, succeeded in bringing communally inclined voters together under the umbrella of a Muslim United Front (MUF) and posed what looked like the biggest electoral threat the National Conference had faced till then. But instead of facing it with his own well proven electoral strength, Farooq Abdullah manipulated the electoral process to deny the Front even that much space to which it was entitled by the support it was able to muster by legitimate electoral means. As subsequent events were to show, neither was the MUF strong enough to defeat the National Conference nor was G.M. Bhatt's personality or programme entirely inimical to the state's larger interests and its accession to India. If Farooq had not cheated MUF out of its due share of seats, which was in any case much less than the legitimate share of the National Conference, the contribution of both leaders and their parties to the politics of the state probably would have been very different from and much better than it came to be.

Taking full advantage of the prostrate people of the state and their disenchantment with New Delhi's and Srinagar's professions of democracy, and playing instead upon the religious sentiments of the Muslims of the state, Pakistan succeeded in sidetracking the admirably secular political and economic struggle begun in Kashmir in the early 1950s by the National Conference. Instead the state became embroiled in a competition between India and Pakistan to show who could create more havoc, and MUF slipped into the fold of the separatists in the Hurriyat conglomerate. This gave the "Farooq family" further scope for convincing Delhi that it was India's only hope in Kashmir, and therefore New Delhi must not look too closely at how the National Conference won elections. The result was as bad as could be expected.

It is from this pit that the electoral process in the state had to be lifted this year before the voter could be persuaded to believe that the Indian Constitution gave him all the full right of a voter in a democracy to elect a government of his choice. The task, difficult in any case because of the communal frenzy Pakistan had whipped up, was made much more so when the Pakistan-based militants turned their well proven prowess as terrorists upon voters. Before polling began in October, they declared that anyone found taking part in the election would be shot, and they backed up the threat with deadly attacks on polling stations and staff. No one was left in any doubt that the staff could hold elections and the people could vote only at serious and clear risk to their lives.

Yet both chose to face the risk. Assisted, no doubt, by the elaborate security at hand but driven mostly by their desire to assert their democratic rights, the people came out in appreciable numbers to vote. Unfortunately they could not do so in some urban concentrations, particularly in Srinagar, which had become the strongholds of armed militancy, and since these were densely populated areas, the overall turnout of voters was affected in parts of Kashmir. Yet the overall turn out was a respectable 45 per cent and even in Kashmir there were areas which registered above 60 per cent polling. The result was the stunning phenomenon, seen for the first time in the state, that the government fell because it had lost the confidence of the people. This restoration and vindication of the electoral process was the first and main aim of the election, and it was met. In an election which was free enough to have brought down the government, the voters gave themselves a house of their choice for the first time in twenty years.

After the election it was argued by some that the result should not be seen as endorsement of the state's accession to India, because people had voted only to unseat an unpopular government. Up to a point this is true. But beyond that it is not. First, no organised group or party or prominent independent candidate campaigned even for a review of the terms of accession, let alone question the act of accession. Second, most of those known to be opposed to the accession were defeated. Third, the largest number of seats in the new house have been won by the National Conference though it has lost its majority, and NC remains firmly committed to the accession. The second biggest bloc is that of the Congress, which is not only a supporter of the accession but a part author of it in the sense that it was the party in power in India when Srinagar asked for accession and New Delhi agreed to it. Fourth, these two parties between them have the majority in the house, with or without counting those who are members of these two parties but stood as independents because they were denied the party ticket. Fifth, the third largest party and the largest from the valley, the People's Democratic Party, is not opposed to the accession but only to ways in which the government has handled the militancy.

But most important is the last and sixth reason. While no one directly raised the issue of accession, it emerged quite significantly as the election campaign developed into a combat between unarmed voters who were determined to vote and the heavily armed militants who were determined to prevent them from doing so. Most of those who boycotted the election by political intention, and all of those who tried violently to intimidate others into boycotting them, were groups and parties known to be against the accession. All those who voted or campaigned in favour of voting were either declared supporters of the Indian connection or were declaring that they were more interested in good governance than in the colour of the government. The declared supporters of the accession have gained a clear majority in the new assembly, and the remaining seats have gone to those who were demanding better governance, not secession.

As the coalition between the Congress and the People's Democratic Party emerged, it showed several other gains as well. It is not only a coalition between two parties but also between the two most important communities and regions of the state. The Congress won more votes and seats in the Hindu majority province of Jammu, and the PDP in the Muslim majority province of Kashmir; and the third province, Ladakh, has never been against the accession. Secondly, the PDP brings to the new government a sharper awareness of the sentiments and grievances of the people of Kashmir and of internal threats to security, and the Congress a broader understanding of the longer term economic and external security needs of the state and the contribution New Delhi can make to meeting them.

That the two are partners in the new government should make it easier for both to understand where the balance should be struck from time to time between, on the one hand, easing political and security restrictions in the state for making life easier for the people, and on the other hand enforcing them for meeting their security needs. A particular illustration is the popular demand in the state that movement of goods and people across the Line of Control in Kashmir should be made easier. It should be. But so long as the Pakistan side of Kashmir has an open border with Pakistan and the Indian side with India, any gates opened between the two sides in the LoC will also become gates between India and Pakistan. Therefore a loose LoC is incompatible with a hard Indo-Pakistan border. The two should be relaxed in matching steps.

But there are also some traps here which must be flagged. The most important among them is the issue of "autonomy". This pit has been dug with equal zeal by the governments in Srinagar and New Delhi. In one of his fits of indiscretion, Farooq Abdullah appears to have gone back on an assurance he had given to the Government of India that while the state assembly must discuss the popular demand for "autonomy", it would not raise any very specific demands until he had consulted New Delhi. Instead he confronted New Delhi with a fully worked out and overloaded charter of demands which had already been adopted by the state assembly. New Delhi's response was also ill-tempered and shortsighted. Instead of reasoning with him and explaining what could be considered and what could not be for the time being, an approach to which he has never failed to respond when his ego and temper have cooled, New Delhi brusquely rejected the report and, as it were, asked him to find his home.

In the process, both sides overlooked the fact that in 1975-76 Sheikh Abdullah and Mrs Indira Gandhi had signed an agreement, however craftily phrased by clever clever people around both leaders, that if requested by the state assembly India would review any extensions of New Delhi's jurisdiction over the state which had been effected during the years that the Sheikh was in prison. Both governments have to find a way out of that pit, dug by both in competitive bad manners. Otherwise both sides will lose the gains they have and the aims desired by them.

A way out exists through three gates. First, Srinagar must realise that the bigger the autonomy it demands from New Delhi the bigger will be the autonomy demanded by Jammu and Ladakh from Srinagar. Second, New Delhi must respond to the new situation created by the recent elections. Just as the Indian military has shown Pakistan can never wrest the state by force, the voters have shown Pakistan cannot get it by political subversion either. Therefore both can revert to the wisdom of the remark by a former Prime Minister of India, Mr Narasimha Rao, that short of secession the sky is the limit for the powers the state can have. Third, both should revert to the enhanced "devolution" envisaged in any honest interpretation of the Indira-Sheikh agreement. That word is limitlessly flexible, and also free of the room for squabbling which exists, and which interested third parties might wish to exploit, over the precise meaning of "autonomy" in a given situation. Such squabbling can re-awaken the ghost of "plebiscite" which the United Nations itself, not India, buried in 1957.

9

Dividing Kashmir?

Mid, 2002

On January 17 this year, General Musharraf "ruled out" the idea floating in India that the half a century old "Kashmir tangle" may be resolved by dividing the state along the present or modified Line of Control. By doing so, the General has done India an unintended favour because it gives India more time to think the idea through.

The idea itself is not new. An American researcher, Dennis Kux, claims Dulles and Nehru agreed in the early 1950s that such a solution might be better than a plebiscite. In 1963, when Sardar Swaran Singh and Mr Z. A. Bhutto, then Foreign Ministers of India and Pakistan, met in Karachi I asked them later the same day whether they had discussed such a partition of Kashmir, and both confirmed they did. On January 20 this year, a former Indian Foreign Secretary, Mr J.N. Dixit, publicly confirmed that he had proposed the idea in 1991 to Mr Nawaz Sharif, then Prime Minister of Pakistan, and a year earlier his predecessor, Mr Muchkund Dubey, had put it to Mr Sharif's predecessor, Benazir Bhutto. Obviously the idea did not prosper at these meetings, because when the Chief Minister of J&K, Mr Farooq Abdullah, repeated it forcefully at a public gathering on January 20 this year, General Musharraf turned it down still more bluntly.

When Sardar Swaran Singh and Mr Bhutto sat down with maps before them in 1963, Bhutto drew a line which would have left only two districts of Jammu for India and put the rest of that province and the whole of Kashmir on the Pakistan side. India suggested a line which was obviously retaliatory because when I asked him what it was, Mr Swaran Singh, with the Indian High Commssioner at that time, Mr G.P. Parthsarthy looking on, indicated one which could have been closer to Rawalpindi than to Srinagar. Of course, the maps had to be folded up immediately, but the exercise proved that what matters is not the idea of division along a line but where the line is drawn. Benazir Bhutto and Mr Nawaz Sharif were non-committal even about the idea according to Mr Dixit.

Considering its pedigree, the idea of some such division is not going to go away any time soon, whether it is pressed by India, or Pakistan, or third parties, and whatever their respective motives for pressing it might be. The approaching elections in the state will make it ring even louder. Therefore official India in the first place, the Indian public in general, and "the people of Kashmir" in particular must urgently consider its pros and cons in the coming weeks.

Many have held it for long that the reason why the Indian army did not push on all the way to the Pakistan border in 1948 is that Sheikh Abdullah was not interested in anything to the west of the proper Kashmir valley, and as soon as that was won back he persuaded Nehru to accept a cease-fire. But even if that story is apocryphal, it is clear that the Kashmiris are much more concerned with the status of the valley than with the fate of PoK. If they got a status for themselves which would satisfy them, they might rather be without the Mirpuri and tribal hordes of PoK and

Pakistan's Northern Territories, which most Kashmiris regard as inferior beings, as the Tajiks and Uzbeks of northern and Shias of western Afghanistan probably regard the Pushtun Taliban of the south.

If that is so, then for a large proportion of Kashmiris what makes them masters of the valley matters more than what happens to PoK, and this proportion could be large enough to constitute the majority in J&K as a whole when added to those in Jammu and Ladakh who favour continued accession of the state to India. So the crucial issue which New Delhi and Srinagar need to explore is not whether to divide the state and if so along what line but what *sustainable* status would the state prefer over conceivable alternatives. This exploration cannot even begin until New Delhi suspends its earlier and brusque rejection of the idea of some form of autonomy for the valley within the Union, and until Srinagar ceases to be cold to autonomy for the three regions within J&K. If a consensus emerged it could impart real meaning to the elections due in the state in the second half of this year.

Without some such possibility, division would make even less sense than the present dispensation in the state. In fact it could dilute the message India, at some cost to itself, has just succeeded in delivering to Pakistan. Despite 1971, the present day Pakistan had continued to believe till yesterday that it has an endless contract on the low cost option of bleeding India without incurring a full scale war, in which the post-71 Pakistan could suffer the same fate as the pre-71 Pakistan did. India has given Pakistan a timely reminder that 1965 was not an exception to the rule. It *is* the rule, that if India is pushed beyond the limits of its tolerance, which is much lower today than in the mid-60's, Pakistan would have to face more than it can handle.

But that message is as instructive, if not more, without shifting the LoC, whether it be shifted with or without the consent of Pakistan. Quite clearly, Pakistan would consent only if it gained something by doing so, but what would India get in exchange ? The American journalist and scholar, Selig Harrison, has just disclosed a private conversation with Mr Advani in which the latter said infiltration of terrorists from Pakistan could be better checked if the LoC were "adjusted". But why would Pakistan help India to check it better ? Of course, Pakistan would happily agree to shifting the Line closer to the valley. But why would India agree to that, even if it got compensating "adjustments" elsewhere in the state ? For instance it would be a questionable bargain for India if it exchanged something in the neighbourhood of the valley for anything to the west of Jammu province where the people are much more in favour of Pakistan than most Kashmiris have ever been.

Some reasonable dividing line would be worth considering if Pakistan could be relied upon, *sincerely,* to respect it as an international border. Can it be ? "Yes", some would say, because of its educative experiences in 1971 and now. But Pakistan's intentions and capability have never been as much of a problem for India as the traditional American myopia has been. Can India hope that America has a better vision now of its real and long term interests in this region ? Even posing these questions underscores the argument that in the time General Musharraf's obduracy has given it, India must clear up its mind about the idea of a new LoC before the dust of the impending elections in the state makes that more difficult than it is already.

10

Cross-roads in Kashmir

Early, 2001

Within three weeks we have had two somewhat differing assessments about the ground situation in Kashmir, not conflicting in substance but in tone and context. On December 20th the Prime Minister was reported as saying in Parliament that though there had been some decline in infiltration it had not been enough, and it had to stop entirely before the "composite dialogue" between India and Pakistan could be resumed. His tone was positive but the substance cautious, and he preferred silence at this stage on the question whether the cease-fire he had announced would be extended or not. This question he parried again on his return from South-East Asia.

The need for caution was reinforced by the Principal Secretary to the Prime Minister, Mr Brijesh Mishra, in Bali, Indonesia, on January 12. While denying that an invitation for talks had been sent to General Parvez Musharaff, Mr Mishra recalled Mr Vajpayee's statement in Parliament that a "conducive atmosphere "was necessary "for things to proceed towards a dialogue on the Kashmir issue." He also expressed concern over an increase in attacks on civilians in Kashmir following India's cease-fire, the attack on the Red Fort by Pakistan-based militants, and their threat to attack the Prime Minister's Office in New Delhi.

But also on January 12, the Chief of the Army Staff, Gen. S. Padmanabhan, chose to go further. While recognising that the decision must rest with government, he clearly urged extension of the cease-fire. "It is a good thing to continue with" he added, as the advantages of doing so far outweighed the disadvantages." And for good measure he added there had been "a sea change in the overall situation", thus virtually recommending an extension.

The contrast between the two assessments is yet another reminder that when the situation is as complicated and the choices as hard as they are in Kashmir, close coordination is needed at the top among those who have to inform, enlighten, prepare public opinion about the decision they might have to take. In any case, the impact of an extension or termination of the cease-fire will be greater if it is announced by the Prime Minister after taking the time he will need to assess all that has happened in and about Kashmir during his absence from India. Critical cross-roads lie beyond any decision the Prime Minister might take about the cease-fire.

In the meantime the drama of the Hurriyat's encounter with Pakistan must unfold itself. The Hurriyat might or might not be as important as, with some assistance from Pakistan, it makes itself out to be. But the outcome of its projected visit to Pakistan could be educative for the visitors as well as the host. The Hurriyat will discover, face to face, how much cooperation it can expect from the militants based it Pakistan, who have bluntly questioned its credentials, including Mr Geelani's. Pakistan will discover from the visitors at first hand what is the strength and what are the implications of the desire for peace which is sweeping the valley. The outcome could offer some straws in the wind which India needs to take note of in shaping its steps as it approaches the cross-roads.

The Hurriyat itself has also compounded its difficulties,

and so has Pakistan. The Hurriyat's strident demands, which it issues as though they were ultimatums, particularly the latest one that either all the members of its executive must be given passports to go to Pakistan or none of them would go, could persuade some exasperated people in Delhi to call its bluff. Pakistan is posturing as though it has invited the Hurriyat as a mediator between India and Pakistan and a partner to a dialogue between the two countries. India has never accepted that position and never will. This could affect the credibility of such counsel as the Hurriyat might wish to offer on its return to India, and that would disappoint those very people whose interests the Hurriyat claims to represent.

Indications are that the desire of the people of Kashmir for peace has grown stronger since the last week of July last year when, bending to as well as reflecting this desire, Abdul Majid Dar, of the Kashmir-based wing of the Hizbul Mujahideen, announced his own startling, unilateral, and unconditional cease-fire. *His* credentials for peace were strongly confirmed when the Pakistan-based wing of the Hizbul Mujahideen (the distinction between the two wings is sometimes missed in media reports) denounced him as a peace monger. New Delhi has also made the assessment that even "the surrendered militants", unpopular though they are with some sections of Kashmiri opinion, are now applauded publicly when they urge peace. Hurriyat leaders cannot be unaware of this fact and cannot afford to be, and one hopes they will also convey it to Pakistan.

For the Indian government too this desire in Kashmir is the star it must always keep within sight as it negotiates the eddies and whirlpools of Kashmiri politics and the broader politics of the sub-continent. As it is, public moods are variable. The mood in Kashmir can change if some unfortunate event occurs. It can, during the panchayat elections, which have begun. It could have, on January 14, when someone fired a rifle grenade at a meeting Chief

Minister Farooq Abdullah was addressing. The grenade fell far away and the police did not have to retaliate, but it could have gone differently.

The government cannot control contingencies which it cannot foresee. But two are clearly visible, and the government needs must prepare itself for them, and the country too. The first is that if the cease-fire is extended and it goes well, it will need to be followed by talks between New Delhi and Srinagar on the extent of the Union Government's jurisdiction over the state, particularly with regard to the extensions of the Union's jurisdiction which were effected during the period when Sheikh Abdullah was under detention. The second is whether India and Pakistan should talk to each other on Kashmir, and if so when and on what basis.

Both contingencies arise inescapably from the fact that cease-fires cannot follow each other in a vacuum. Either they must be followed up by further progress, whether on the New Delhi-Srinagar axis or on the New Delhi-Islamabad axis, and preferably on both. Or they must come to an end, with whatever the consequences of that may be. Some follow-up steps are discernible, and they have a respectable lineage. Some steps on the New Delhi-Srinagar axis are to be found in the accord signed by Mrs Gandhi with Sheikh Abdullah in 1974, which envisaged some restoration of the autonomy J&K had within the Indian Union when the Sheikh was the Chief Minister of the state. Those on the second axis have been lucidly spelt out in the Sheikh's letter to Mrs Gandhi in 1976, and were more recently restated by Farooq Abdullah when he talked about the Line of Control becoming more like an international border. The basis for discussing these and other steps has been cast in cement by the Lahore documents, which neither India nor Pakistan should try to by-pass.

But the follow up on each axis requires changes in the present positions of the governments of the Union and the state on one axis, and of the governments of India and Pakistan on the other. None of the three will find the changes easy to make, and all three will find them difficult to sell to their respective people. The only hope of selling them lies in the hard fact of life that anything is acceptable if the only alternative to it is worse, and the worst possible alternative for all three of them is indefinite continuation of the recent and the current tribulations of all three.

11

"Cease-fire" with Teeth

Early, 2001

Half-way through the three-month "cease-fire" announced by Prime Minister Vajpayee at the end of February, the Government of India has offered a basis on which both sides can hold fire for much longer while talks proceed for something more lasting. That is the crux of the long and formal statement issued by the Government of India on the evening of April 5.

As expected, the first responses to it have been largely negative. Similar initiatives about Kashmir have yielded so little so often in the past that hope of something dramatic now is faint. And it can evaporate altogether if too much is expected too soon in a situation in which, learning from past failures, both sides may prefer – as they should — to take only one step at a time. But this time there are some changes too which should not be overlooked. They can make a difference if they are given a chance.

Take the first change. In inviting "a political dialogue with all sections of the peace loving people of the state (of Jammu and Kashmir)", the government has specifically included "those who are currently outside it." This could mean something as little as inviting Kashmiris, whether Hindus or Muslims, who used to live in the state but had to migrate "outside" because of the militancy. But it could also mean two more things, which would widen the participation of "the state" in the "political dialogue".

The phrase could cover separatists who migrated from the state because of their opposition to the state's accession to India. At the minimum this could mean those who are now "outside" both India and Pakistan. More hopefully it could mean those who belong to the state but are now in Pakistan, including those parts of "the state" which are under the occupation of Pakistan. Two facts should be recalled in this context.

First, when Abdul Majid Dar, a senior leader of the Hizbul Mujahideen who has lately been living on the Indian side of the state, announced a unilateral cease-fire in the last week of July, he was hailed by the people of the Kashmir valley, including those elements of the Hizb who like him have been living in the valley for some time past. On the other hand he was denounced by those Kashmiri elements of the Hizb who live in Pakistan and are possibly controlled by it, and they ultimately succeeded in scuttling Majid Dar's move. Ever since then it has appeared likely that there are Kashmiries living in Pakistan and in the Pakistan controlled parts of "the state" who would support a move like Majid Dar's if they were free to do so, or if it were floated by New Delhi itself as a step towards a wider and more purposeful dialogue.

Second, it was with an eye on them that some weeks ago a former Chief Minister of Jammu Kashmir, Mr Ghulam Mohammad Shah, once an estranged relative of the present Chief Minister, Mr Farooq Abdullah, invited the more prominent among them to a conference in Jammu. The conference collapsed because the Government of India declined to give visas to them. That was a mistake. But it is quite possible that they would get visas if they agreed to come for talks initiated by the Government of India, and not by a one time opponent of Farooq Abdullah, who for years has been the strongest Kashmiri supporter of the state's accession to India.

New Delhi should have every reason to be glad if people from across the Line of Control also responded to its invitation to talks. Whatever be the mindset with which they came, India should explore their choices too. Those in official positions in PoK might not be allowed by Pakistan to come, but non-official individuals and organisations might find it easier. For this reason it is good that the invitation has cast its net wide and has addressed all "peace loving people of the state" and all kinds of organisations " from all the regions of the state", including "political parties, non-government organisations, trade unions, and social and religious bodies".

The first reaction of the Hurriyat's present President, Abdul Ghani Bhatt, has been that India must first allow the Hurriyat to send a team of its own choice to Pakistan.[1] Such a visit might have been easier for New Delhi to accept if, with the assistance of some members of the Hurriyat, Pakistan had not insisted on its interpretation that the team would be visiting Pakistan at the invitation of Pakistan and as a mediator between India and Pakistan in a tripartite process. Such an interpretation is totally unacceptable to India, and if the Hurriyat were to insist on its acceptance by India as a condition for agreeing to a dialogue with New Delhi then it will simply have to exclude itself from the proposed dialogue. India also cannot accept Abdul Ghani Lone's position, recently stated publicly, that the Hurriyat alone can represent Kashmir.[2]

But here also there are two facts which are less discouraging. First, while complaining that the Hurriyat had not been "informed" of the proposed talks, Lone is also reported to have added that if steps were taken in that direction, presumably meaning that if the Hurriyat were formally informed of the talks and invited to them, "we will give a positive response."[3] This "step" is a simple one and New Delhi should take it, and soon. Second, there is nothing in the Indian statement of April 5 which would prevent the Hurriyat from asking for a visit to Pakistan in the course of the talks, or even at the beginning if it so desired. Since the Government of India has said that there should be no pre-conditions to the talks, it can no more exclude such a request by the Hurriyat at the talks than the Hurriyat can lay down prior acceptance of the proposed visit as a condition for the talks to begin. The agenda proposed for the talks, "Peace, and how it might be attained", and "all aspects bearing on this theme" is too broad, inclusive, and flexible for anyone either to insist on the inclusion of any proposition in the talks or to insist on its exclusion.

The tone about Pakistan is more nuanced in this Indian statement than in some earlier ones, though the substance remains the same. India acknowledges that Pakistan has been proposing talks, and India "reaffirms it faith in such a dialogue" (though it would be hard for India to substantiate the sentence in the statement that there have been "frequently repeated requests from Pakistan that they are eager for a dialogue with India on J&K". There have been 'demands' from Pakistan in plenty. But "frequently repeated requests" ?). In any case the old conditions for talks with Pakistan remain in place, that is insistence on its "curbing cross border terrorism and putting an end to ...vicious anti-Indian propaganda", and it is clear from this new initiative that for the time being at any rate India is going to concentrate harder on talks with J&K than with Pakistan.

The statement also makes a clear effort to end the confusion which has existed in the media and in the public mind about the phrase "cease-fire", which has been used both frequently and wrongly. More accurate though cumbersome is the phrase India has consistently used in and since its own first announcement of a "cease-fire", namely "non-initiation" of any action by the security forces on their own. What that means precisely is that the security forces will not begin any action unless forced to retaliate against any hostile action by the militants. Unfortunately, after the misleading phrase came to be used by senior ranks in the armed forces too, even retaliatory action became slack. This made the militants more bold and they carried out some daring raids in the course of March and earlier.

More recently the confusion was cleared and retaliatory actions by the security forces were resumed. But because they had not been undertaken for some time, when they were they looked harsher than they were, and were resented more than when they used to be more customary. This made it easier for the separatists to work up public demonstrations, until the mood for peace generated in the public by and since Majid Dar's first announcement of a "cease-fire" began to look all but dead, and in the rest of India too opposition to the whole peace process became more vocal and widespread.

In more recent days retaliatory actions have been as frequent as the provocation for them has been, and have also become more effective, and now the government's statement has made the issue more bluntly clear. It says "the security forces have been directed to vigorously conduct operations against those who disturb the peace and victimise the innocent people of J&K, while at the same time ensuring that the population at large is spared undue hardships and harassment."

All this is as it should be. But the government's efforts have yet to regain the credibility they had when, just under a year ago, the government responded correctly and quickly to the initiative taken by Majid Dar. There are two main reasons for this decline. The first and more serious one is that some of the government's decisions have been patently wrong, as two examples will show. First, the brusque and almost insulting manner in which the Government of India rejected the "autonomy report" presented to it by Farooq Abdullah. The point is not whether the report demanded more autonomy than it should have or more than the Union Government could have conceded. The point is that instead of discussing the demand and explaining to the state's Chief Minister how far it could be conceded and why not more, the report was summarily thrown out. Second, refusal of passports to those whom the Hurriyat wanted to send to

Pakistan, and refusal of visas to those invited by Mr G.M. Shah for the all state conference proposed by him. Again, the point is not whether the passports or the visas should have been denied or not. But the delays, the confusion and a distinct lack of courtesy with which such decisions should be taken. Such delays and ineptitude took a heavy toll when the New Delhi delayed its response to the Hurriyat's demand that the government should clarify whether the talks proposed by Prime Minister last summer would be within or outside the Constitution. The clarification the Prime Minister did ultimately give in the Lok Sabha was eminently sensible, sincere and convincing. But the time it took to come became an opportunity for Pakistan and its supporters in India to foul up the air irretrievably.

To recall these incidents is exercise enough for pointing out what should be done or not if the new initiative by the government is to yield what the government expects it to.

References

1. *The Hindu*, New Delhi, April 7, 01.
2. *The Times of India*, April 7, 01.
3. *The Times of India*, April 6, 01.

12

Hurriyat in a Changing Role

Early, 2001

From the time when the Hurriyat began to show an interest in taking a delegation to Pakistan a couple of years ago, it has been caught in a game invented by Pakistan. Until lately, the Hurriyat had failed to see that in this game it would be a pawn, not a player. It failed because through most of its early and formative years it had been Pakistan's political platform in Kashmir, the political arm of most of the underground militants who were waging an armed war against India with the active support of the Pakistan army. Therefore it did not look critically at Pakistan's manoevures. Those were the years in which Hurriyat leaders during their visits to Delhi became, and were happy to be, prize exhibits at functions at the Pakistan High Commission, particularly on Pakistan's national day, while their distance from India's Republic Day celebrations and other such Indian occasions was conspicuous.

On one occasion some years ago they became, perhaps unwittingly, tools for the Pakistan High Commission for slighting India in a way which would have merited the Commissioner being summoned to the Foreign Office the next day. For this reason few in India were surprised to see that the Hurriyat was more than willing to play Pakistan's game, particularly during the years when Sayed Ali Shah Geelani was its chairman. There was little that India could do about it except to keep the Hurriyat at arm's length. But this suited Pakistan. It was able to show the people of Kashmir that the Hurriyat had no influence with New Delhi and they had no alternative to the jehad waged by heavily armed militants pushed into Kashmir by Pakistan, even though their non-Kashmiri persona grated on the nerves of Kashmiris.

But in the recent election for the next President of the Hurriyat, Geelani was defeated by other leaders of the organisation. Geelani denounces them now as "secular" because they do not see the "Kashmir problem" as religious. But they are slowly succeeding in doing two things. They are rescuing Kashmir's own interests from the coils of Pakistan's confrontation with India, and they are carving out a role for the Hurriyat as a constructive factor both in the affairs of Jammu and Kashmir and as a possible interlocutor for India and Pakistan. Their demand that the Government of India should let them send a delegation to Pakistan is, among others, a part of the new role. But this does not suit Pakistan. As a political entity based in the soil and society of Kashmir, where priorities are changing in response to the growing desire among the people for peace and order, Hurriyat could become a less reliable instrument for Pakistan than militants nurtured in the currents of jehad which are sweeping through Pakistan.

Therefore Pakistan is trying to undercut the new self-image of the Hurriyat by doing four things simultaneously, though not all of them are mutually complimentary. First, through Geelani and such non-Kashmiri militant organisations as are thoroughly committed to Pakistan, it is running down the Hurriyat's proposed visit to Pakistan as a useless exercise. Second, it is portraying the visit as a Kashmiri response to an invitation by Pakistan, and therefore more an instrument of Pakistan's diplomacy than a Kashmiri initiative. Third, it is claiming that the delegation would come as the sole representative of Kashmir. And fourth, its mission would be to mediate between India and Pakistan and to set up a tripartite meeting between India, Pakistan and Kashmir.

Pakistan had been projecting this picture for some time in various direct and indirect statements. But it did so more formally in a statement dated December 2 last year, to which it has been since referring as a definitive formulation of its position on the Hurriyat. This also strengthened, on the one hand, Geelani's insistence that he should be in the Hurriyat delegation, and on the other hand India's reluctance to agree to that. There are many things in that statement which are wholly unacceptable to India. But more relevant here is what it says about the Hurriyat and its intended visit.

It says "In order to enable the representatives of the Kashmiri people to participate in the dialogue" (with India, which the statement proposes in an earlier paragraph) "the Government of Pakistan extends an invitation to the Executive Committee of the All Parties Hurriyat Conference, the leader of the Kashmiri freedom struggle, for consultations to prepare the ground for a tripartite process of negotiations ...." Before coming to that point the statement accuses India of "repression and violence".

If such had also been the Hurriyat's view of its proposed delegation, India would have had nothing to do with it. India would have only reiterated its initial view that : first, some of the Hurriyat's top leaders have already been to Pakistan individually; second, others already had visas and could go there individually if they wished to do so; third, still others who wished to go could also apply for passports, and their applications would be considered in the usual course; but, fourth, if they wished to go there as a delegation representing Kashmir, then the proposal would have to be considered on its own merits. As for a "tripartite process", India's position for some decades now has been that talks with Pakistan can only be bilateral, with no mediatory role for anyone, and least of all for any part of India. It is a different matter whether India should or should not agree that there is a dispute over Kashmir, as Pakistan and the leader of the Pakistan based Hizbul Mujahideen demand it should. But India would never accept any role for Kashmir which requires that India accept that Kashmir is not a part of India.

With such a projection by Pakistan and such a response by India, the Hurriyat's proposal would have remained in the deep freeze which descended on Indo-Pakistan relations in the wake of Pakistan's misadventure in Kargil. This would have disappointed the Hurriyat and the growing number of people in J&K and the rest of India who have been watching the Hurriyat's recent evolution with sympathetic interest. It would have suited Pakistan to the extent that it would have helped Pakistan to tell Kashmir that the Hurriyat was a non-starter as an alternative to jehad. But it would have done little else, except to condemn Kashmir to further killings while the jehadies and Indian security forces slugged it out. But the outlook changed when, in spite of Geelani, the Executive Committee of the Hurriyat took an interesting new stance in the resolution it adopted at its meeting in Srinagar on February 12, distancing itself from the Pakistani position of December 2.

First, the resolution avoids all those derogatory references which Pakistan made on December 2 to various aspects of India's policies and actions in Kashmir, and particularly to India's announcement (wrongly described as "cease-fire") that it will not initiate military actions for another month, till the end of the Ramzan. The resolution called this a "positive approach". Second, it called for "the creation of a peaceful atmosphere" (India's phrase is "conducive"), which it described as "imperative in order to find a permanent and peaceful solution of the Kashmir problem". Third, it described the creation of such an atmosphere as the reason why "the Hurriyat" (not Pakistan) "has moved a proposal to visit Pakistan." Fourth, in contrast with Mr Geelani and certain militant and religious organisations in Pakistan, the resolution firmly described "the problem" as political and not religious. Fifth, while blaming India for not following up on the " cease-fire" , and describing Pakistan's response to it as "positive", it blamed "certain people" in Pakistan too and not only in India for trying "to influence the decision making authority of the Hurriyat too" and declared it would not "accept influence from anybody". It made no reference to any "tripartite process" as the goal of its proposed visit to Pakistan, and claimed no exclusive right to represent the people of Kashmir.

It is quite possible that as these signals of change in the Hurriyat register in Delhi, the ground will be cleared for it to send a delegation to Pakistan, particularly if Geelani steps aside or is replaced by his leader, G.M. Bhat, President of the Jamat-I-Islami, which Geelani represents in the Hurriyat. But many questions stand as yet between that event and any fruitful outcome of the Hurriyat's visit. To be tested in the next few days is the question how well will Indian security forces reconcile their twin duties in this context : to deal effectively with the threats and actions of the heavily armed militants from Pakistan, and at the same time to avoid unnecessary loss of civilian lives, which is the declared purpose of the Indian "cease-fires". In the past the militants have been able to provoke such actions by the security forces as came close to derailing the peace sentiment in Kashmir. It may be useful to ban anyone from carrying illegal arms. It will not be easy to implement the ban but anyone still carrying them would become a self-declared offender and preventive action against him a legitimate precaution.

To be tested over a slightly longer period is the question how are the peace tables to be shaped, should the need for building some arise after the Hurriyat visit to Pakistan. The Indo-Pakistan dialogue will of course require only a table with two sides to it and two flags on it. But whether that table comes to be needed one day or not, there will have to be one in New Delhi or Srinagar – and where out of these two places; and why not also in Jammu and Leh by turns ? – for a postmortem of the Hurriyat's visit and for considering what other steps should follow. Should New Delhi (or Srinagar ?) also invite the different regions of J&K on the Pakistan side of the Line of Control to send their representatives ? The regions on both sides of the Line have an interest in autonomy.

That of course raises a number of tough subjects both for New Delhi and Srinagar. Both capitals will have to live down the blunders they made last summer in handling the issue of autonomy. Srinagar blundered in not living up its assurance to New Delhi that the state's Autonomy Report would be first discussed with New Delhi and then debated in the state assembly. New Delhi then blundered even more by rejecting the Report in a manner so abrupt that it was insulting. How will New Delhi then offer any level of autonomy to any government in Srinagar which it refused to concede to Farooq Abdullah's National Conference, which has more outspokenly supported accession to India than any political party in Kashmir? And how will any party at present opposed to the National Conference accept a level which was too low even for the National Conference to accept?

However the Hurriyat may fare in its parleys in Pakistan, how will it fare in such parleys as will have to take place in Srinagar whether it goes to Pakistan or not ? How will it find accommodation with the National Conference, which New Delhi cannot and will not jettison ? And how will both find accommodation with the fascinating new actor which has surface in J&K, the very large number of panches who have been elected in the hugely successful panchayat elections which have already taken place in some parts of the state and will be completed in other parts before long ? The voters have neither obeyed the militants nor the Hurriyat, both of whom had given calls for a boycott of the elections. The voter turn out, largely genuine, exceeded levels witnessed in many elections in the rest of India. Have they given a powerful new platform for the National Conference, which had defied both the militants and the Hurriyat in holding the elections? Or have they themselves become a powerful new platform ?

One mentions all these questions not only because they cannot be ignored for long but also because finding answers to them will require that the changes taking place in the Hurriyat will have to go on, and also spread to other political arenas. The consequences may overshadow any discussions which may take place between the governments of India and Pakistan, if any do at all.

13

Jehad, Illusions, and Lakshman

Late, 2000

Many countries have experienced violence which is related to Islam, whether committed by supporters or opponents of "Jehad", and irrespective of whether Jehad means peaceful service of the faith, as supporters, quoting texts, insist it does; or it means service with the sword, as opponents, quoting history, insist it becomes. The violence has recently occurred in the Philippines in the east, in Indonesia and Malaysia in the south, in Kashmir, Xinjiang, Chechniya in the north, Algeria in the west. It has flared up most within and between the core countries of the faith, some of them its cradle and the scene of its greatest achievements, such as Iran, Iraq, Egypt.

The consequences affect the future of Islam.. On the one hand the world has become more aware of Islam than it used to be, adherence to it has become harder where it used to mild, as among South-east Asian Malays, its codes have become stricter, as in Iran for some time and more recently in Afghanistan. It has probably struck deeper roots in tribal Africa, where a more systematic Islam has gained ground from whatever existed before. On the other hand it has stopped making the inroads it made among Black

Americans in the days when Cassius Clay became Mohammed Ali and Malcolm X a media mystery. What is more important, its growth path has been affected.

In the past, Islam had moved forward on two legs : on the appeal of the principles of the faith, which are robustly progressive and just; and on the organised politico-military power of many Muslim majority countries. But both legs have grown weaker. The appeal of the principles has been clouded by the manner in which they have been practiced by the fratricidal fanatic, who pitted Muslim against Muslim and swept many of them out of the mansions of the faith with the broom of narrow doctrines. In Afghanistan they have crossed all limits of reason, and they have aroused suspicion and resistance in the Central Asian states, which were once seen as its most promising new pastures. The phrase "Islamic fundamentalist" has become associated with something "Inquisitorial".

Its internal feuds have taken a heavier toll of Islam than the opposition of "infidels". For a time this fact was obscured by the mountain of "petro dollars", which was counted as part of Islamic power. But the mountain was soon eroded by conflicts between some of the most prominent Islamic countries, which converted their oil wealth into a gold mine for the arms industry of non-Islamic countries, including the "Great Satan", as America was called by the fanatic. In some other Islamic countries the legendary profligacy of the rulers made paupers out of princes and crass policies drained away much of the political and military prowess they had once added to Islam:

Nearer home is the interesting case of Pakistan. Its former President, Zia, dreamed of building an Islamic empire stretching from its borders with India to the Russian border. The dream became a bitter illusion as Afghanistan, the first stepping stone to that empire, was reduced to rubble by wars between zealots. Instead, Pakistan became a wounded battle ground for clashes between different brands of warriors of the faith, and Zia's domestic dream, "Nizam-e-Mustafa", became an embarrassment for the more forward looking Muslims.

This is the troubled background against which the Muslims of India have to work out their own destiny as the world's largest population of Muslims who are a minority in their country, and also the second largest population of Muslims in any country. History has not made life easy for them, neither the earlier history, before India became independent; nor the earlier history of independent India; nor the history of the future as it is emerging from the womb of the present. Every community, whether it is in majority or minority, rightly cherishes its "golden age." But the trouble is that memories of the past become a liability if they delay viable settlements with the present. India is in danger of proving this to be true though the golden ages of both Hindus and Muslims are equally unrelated to the present condition and prospects of both. Similarly irrelevant though too recent to forget easily is the more painful reality that in the eyes of the majority of Muslims in what later became Pakistan, and in the eyes of the majority of Hindus of what continued to be India, the other became the "other nation" of the two-nation theory which hijacked history in the 1940s.

It would have been easier for the Hindus and Muslims of independent India to see the irrelevance of this whole chain of earlier events if Indian politics had retained the secular temper they had during the first two decades of independence under the umbrella of the Congress. But on account of yet another chain of events, which climaxed during the Emergency but lingered for long afterwards, the Congress went into a steep and now all but irreversible decline. The next two decades, the 70's and 80s, had a strong strand of secular politics, the protest of the lower and poorer castes and classes. But although it was a secular strand, and although the poor and deprived are at least as high a proportion of the Muslim totality as of the Hindu, the strand failed to evoke as strong a Muslim participation as it should have. If Muslims joined Dalit movements at all it was more because these were opposed to Hindu orthodoxy than because they demanded economic justice.

In the 90s BJP became a major force among Hindus, and that of course was anathema to the Muslim. Therefore for close upon thirty years Hindus and Muslims reached out to each other only minimally across the communal divide between them. That helped Pakistan to score the only success it can claim over the last few decades, that it was able to add a stronger communal twist to the Kashmir issue by giving it the face of Jehad, and thereby succeeded in making the chill in Hindu-Muslim relations that much deeper throughout the country.

What is the future of that success ? It depends upon how the two newest factors in Indian politics play out. On the one hand we have certain positive factors. First a realisation within BJP that it can broaden and improve its parliamentary role only by widening its base among the Dalits and Muslims. Hence the first ever election of a Dalit, Bangaru Lakshman, to the highest office of BJP, its President. In its own way and at its own level this is as novel and creative an experience for BJP as such as the election of Mr Narayanan, of the scheduled castes, as the President of the Republic is for India as a whole. Second, a conspicuous reaching out to Muslims by Lakshman. Realising the importance of this development, unprecedented in recent times, at least one notable Muslim, Maulana Wahiduddin, has called it "the biggest opportunity for Muslims", and a Muslim scholar and commentator, Mashirul Hasan, has argued that the opportunity should be given a chance. His reasoning has the obvious background that if Lakshman gets sandwiched between opposition by BJP's traditionalists and a frosty response by Muslims, his initiative might peter out. Third, if the emerging thaw in Kashmir succeeds it could undo the damage done by the Jehadi twist.

But on the other hand there is also the dismal fact that by and large the Muslim response has been sceptical if not outright negative, and amounts to saying that Lakshman's first step may be all right but we cannot welcome it until he takes the tenth, or that we cannot support him since that would help BJP gain the support of liberal Hindus, never mind the good it might do to relations between the majority and minority communities. Therefore it cannot be ruled out that the sceptical Muslim and the orthodox Hindu may jointly nip "the biggest opportunity" in the bud. How that would benefit the world's largest Muslim minority remains to be seen.

14

Hizbul's Reasons and Prospects

Mid, 2000

In the week since the Hizbul Mujahideen (HM) offered unconditional talks for a cease-fire, it has become possible to speculate (no more, yet) upon its reasons for doing so. The speculation is encouraged by a number of quick developments during the week. First, the Union Government made an equally unconditional and measured response. Second, HM remained firm on the offer despite strong and public disapproval in Pakistan. Third, despite the bloody provocation of the murder over 100 unarmed and innocent Indians, New Delhi remained fully responsive to HM's offer. Four, the modalities proposed by HM for ceasing-fire are realistic and reasonable. Five, Prime Minister Vajpayee has repeatedly given top priority to ending the alienation of the Kashmiri people in addition to countering militancy. Six, full cooperation has come from Farooq Abdullah despite the unwisely abrupt and humiliating rejection of the Autonomy Report by the Union Government, and despite the suspicion that Pakistan had instigated the cease-fire offer only to sideline the autonomy alternative. There have rarely been so many positive straws within so few days.

Five possible reasons for HM's offer stand out against

this background. First, the dominance of non-Kashmiris, particularly Afghan militants, which Pakistan has been increasingly imposing for a long time upon Kashmiris and which the latter resent. Second, the slow but steady turn of the Kashmiri tide from accession to Pakistan to independence, which is more popular with Kashmiri militants than with those who are more blatantly backed by Pakistan. Third, the widening gap between HM and the militancy control council in Pakistan, as shown in the council's and the Lashkar-i-Toiba's strong denunciation of the cease-fire offer. Fourth, the increasingly obvious futility of militancy as a way of getting India out of Kashmir, and the high cost of the futility. Fifth, the growing international disapproval of the militancy itself and its aggressive use as a tool by Pakistan against India.

And all these causes suddenly gained added edge when, in recent weeks, the prospect of autonomy, be it within India, proved so popular in the valley. If our own cabinet had not been so insensitive to it the agenda today would not have been how to reach a cease-fire but how to balance Kashmir's aspiration for more autonomy within the Union with Jammu's and Ladakh's aspirations for the same within J&K. That would have simultaneously served the interests of the Union, the state, the regions, and taken the country closer to the goal now defined by the Prime Minister as ending Kashmiri alienation.

If all that is now water over the dam, what are the prospects today ? Perhaps it is better to ask first what the prospects are NOT today, before asking what they might become tomorrow. Some limits are obvious. India will not agree - not yet — to make Pakistan a third party to the talks with HM. Nor will India concede to HM, in the present circumstances, what it refused on 4th July to Farooq Abdullah, the stoutest Kashmiri advocate of the state's continued accession to India. Nor is HM so much at the end of its tether that it will be content with sops. Yet the behaviour of both sides behind the scenes indicates a shared realisation that time is needed to hammer out a reliable cease-fire protocol.

Therefore nothing dramatically final will happen because of the expiry of the deadline of 5 pm on August 8 set by HM. Neither a breakdown nor a breakthrough. There might be an interruption for stocktaking, which may look like a collapse. But HM did not come thus far only to go back empty handed and to stand in shame before those who have slammed it for offering a cease-fire in the first place. Nor did the Union Government risk turmoil in its own ranks or in Kashmir on the assumption, unwarranted in any case, that HM is too tired now to carry on and will accept unreasonable terms. Both sides will try to show such success as they can, and at least will not shut the door on such future possibilities as may arise, now that the largest Kashmiri organisation of militancy has changed the scene by taking this unprecedented step, and Prime Minister Vajpayee has changed it by redefining the government's goal in Kashmir as ending the alienation of the people of the state from the rest of the country. Progress may follow a zig zag path, three steps forward alternating with two backwards, as happened on Tuesday evening. But dead ends may not become permanent even though HM has violated its own offer of unconditional talks for a cease-fire by imposing upon it the condition later that Pakistan must be made a party to the talks

But new methods will be needed for future possibilities, so that several approaches may work symbiotically, not at cross purposes. A dependable cease-fire, with the modalities as transparent as security reasons allow but without necessarily calling for changes in political aims, will be obviously the first step, with as many militant outfits joining in as may accept the modalities. If the desire of the people of the state for safety from guns was the main push behind even such a large organisation as HM then its force cannot be ignored by other organisations also, and the price the violators may have to pay in terms of the public's disapproval can be a strong disincentive for violations. Plus of course the obvious fact that only in conditions of at least relative peace can further strategies be thought out by those for whom violence has not become an ideology, by whatever name it may be called.

Second, we should get away from the present disruptive debate over whether a discussion about modalities is within the constitution or not. The Union's or the state's constitution neither allows nor bars an exploratory discussion on anything. Their limits or their latitudes are relevant only to such specifics as the exploration may suggest, and to such steps as may be considered for implementing the specifics. Both constitutions also have some flexibility and leeway to permit tomorrow what they might not today, provided the permission is sought for objectives which have sufficient support for permissible amendments. Therefore the government and its critics, and to some extent HM as well, are needlessly tying themselves up in knots in demanding or refuting that the discussions be within or outside the two constitutions. They can save their breath till the need arises for it. That is why the statement by the Prime Minister in Parliament on Monday on this point was as timely as it was clear and emphatic.

There is a serious flaw in the state government's Autonomy Report insofar as it demands unilaterally that the Union Government should withdraw such extensions of its jurisdiction over the state which the Union Parliament legislated after the arrest of Sheikh Abdullah in 1953, its argument being that with the Sheikh in prison the state's government and legislature had lost the mandate of the people. There is a grain of political truth in that but not an iota of legal or constitutional justification. So long it has been formed in conformity with the law, a government does not cease to be legal merely because it is less popular than the preceding government.

But there would be no such flaw in either of two courses. Either the state government should seek validity of the Autonomy Report not in its adoption by the state assembly but in such consensus as may emerge over it in discussions between the two governments. Or it should seek redress not through the Autonomy Report but through reconsideration, jointly by the two governments, of the Accord jointly signed in the mid-1970s by Sheikh Abdullah and Mrs Indira Gandhi, and through such implementation of the existing Accord or such enlargement of it as the two governments can agree on.

But while all these considerations and reconsiderations may help, prospects for the future do not depend so much on the constitutionality or legality of one option or another but on the test now rightly laid down by the Prime Minister for all options : which one, however novel or innovative its legal or constitutional status, will help more in ending the alienation of the people of the state from the rest of the country, and in ending the new alienation that has raised its head within the state, the alienation of the valley from the other two regions, Jammu and Ladakh.

15

Hope and Despair in Kashmir

Late, 2000

For several weeks now Jammu and Kashmir have been hanging between hope and despair, caught between the obduracy being shown by the Hizbul Mujahideen and New Delhi. The Hizb is demanding recognition from New Delhi of something which is so obvious and established that it needs no fresh certificate of recognition. New Delhi is refusing to see that there is no harm in giving a certificate which may be unnecessary but can be potently useful.

The Mujahideen want India to say that there can be no 'final settlement' of the future of the state without talks with Pakistan. But this is obvious. No settlement can be 'final' unless it also settles the future of that part of the state which has been captured by Pakistan, and that can be done only through talks with Pakistan. India has also recognised this in agreements with Pakistan, at Simla in 1971 and at Lahore in 1998. This is a settled fact.

But reiteration of the obvious and the settled can do no harm if it can open new possibilities of peace. The Hizbul has offered three. First, it will renew the offer it made on July 24 that it will unilaterally observe an interim cease-fire for three months while it negotiated a longer term agreement.. Second, this time it will try to bring other militant groups to the same position. Third, it will accept that Pakistan need not be made a party to the talks immediately but at some later stage, which obviously means 'the stage' would have to be acceptable to New Delhi also, not only to the Hizb.

The Hizbul Mujahideen would be on test on all three counts if New Delhi only reiterated what it is committed to already. First, it would have to restore and observe the interim cease-fire. If it failed to do so, or again wriggled out on flimsy grounds or on second thoughts or under pressure from Pakistan, it would fall foul of the desire for peace which is widespread among the people of the state, particularly including the people of the valley. It is this desire more than anything else which had compelled the Hizb to make its original offer, and this compulsion is still in place.

Second, the Hizb would have to prove its power to persuade the other militant groups, or else re-assess its equation with them, while the people of the state made their own reassessment of the claims of the Hizb and the intentions of the other militant groups. Third, the Hizb would have to shoulder the onus of persuading Pakistan to wait in the wings while it negotiated a cease-fire with New Delhi, and then to persuade Pakistan to accept such accord as the Hizb may reach with New Delhi for continuing the cease-fire. If Pakistan refused, it would have to explain itself to that large segment of the people of the valley who had rejoiced when the Hizb took the initiative for an interim cease-fire.

If cease-fire negotiations began again they would have a better start than last July. At that time they faced an immediate problem : how would the Indian security forces distinguish between those who accepted the interim cease-fire and those who did not. But reports suggest the problem was solved by the Hizbul negotiator, Qureshi, agreeing that Hizb militants would remain in their hideouts during the cease-fire.

India would also have more legitimate grounds for

distinguishing between those with whom it agreed to talk and those with whom it did not. More legitimate than that it was willing to talk with the Hizbul Mujahideen but not with the 'military regime' in Islamabad, or willing to talk with those whom Home Minister Advani described as "our own people" but not with others. It would be a distinction between those who had and those who had not offered or accepted the cease-fire. But if Pakistan and others offered or accepted it too, there would be no reason for not talking with them as well at some stage. The scene would change dramatically, for the better.

More immediately to the point would be the difference between the two sections of the Hizb (and corresponding sections of the Jamat-e-Islami). The Hizb (and the Jamat) section residing in the Indian side of Kashmir, including such important Hizb leaders as Majid Dar, Fazal Qureshi, Masood (and the Jamat leader Ghulam Mohammad Bhat) continue to support a cease-fire despite reprimands from the Pakistan-based Hizb section, including the overall Hizb commander, Salaudin, who resides in Pakistan (or is held there as a section of Kashmiris believe).

The gulf between the two sections of the Hizbul Mujahideen is sometimes blurred when Indian media fail to make it clear whether what they are saying about the Hizb concerns or comes from one or the other section. But the gulf is real, and persists. The Hizb in the Indian side is more directly exposed to the desire of the people of the valley for a respite from the killings (by whichever side) and is therefore more sincere in its desire for a cease-fire. On the other hand the earlier cease-fire, announced by Majid Dar, was scuttled by Salaudin and other leaders of the Hizbul section which lives in Pakistan and is engaged (ensnared ?) in Pakistan's games against India. The two sections are agreed on demanding that India must accept that Pakistan is a party to this dispute, but it is very likely that their reasons are different.

Majid Dar and his colleagues could be demanding

recognition of Pakistan as a party to the dispute so that they may have some gain in hand to justify renewal of their cease-fire initiative. The section residing in Pakistan could well be demanding it in order to dissuade Pakistani from scuttling it again. But be that is it may, three things stand out. First, the Hizb section of this side continues to talk in favour of a cease-fire despite instructions to the contrary from the Salaudin camp. Second, Pakistan has been given reason enough to realise that far from gaining anything it has hurt itself in the eyes of the world, including American, and perhaps Kashmiri eyes too, by suppressing Majid Dar's initiative. And third and most important, New Delhi has been given reasons enough to realise that it would lose nothing but gain some by encouraging the initiative with a statement which would be harmless at worst and could be potent at best.

16

Changes in Kashmir

Late, 2000

Speaking in Srinagar, the Chief Minister of Jammu and Kashmir, Mr Farooq Abdullah, said on October 12 he was confident that talks for a fresh cease-fire would begin soon, and hopeful that they would not fail. Two days later the Union Home Minister, Mr Advani, gave a pessimistic assessment. He said in a television interview that cease-fires would not work unless Pakistan changed its mind, because it would scuttle the next cease-fire also as it did the last.

The two leaders were not really contradicting each other. They were only talking of two different things. Farooq Abdullah was talking about what he hoped those Hizbul leaders and militants would do who are based on the Indian side of the Line of Control, and who had announced the earlier cease-fire, on July 24. Mr Advani was referring to Salauddin, the overall commander of the Hizbul Mujahideen, who is based in Islamabad and was pressured by Pakistan to withdraw the cease-fire. Both Mr Abdullah and Mr Advani are quite possibly right.

The growing Kashmiri desire for peace may again weigh with the Hizb who are based in the valley and there may well be what Abdullah calls "some rethinking" among the Hizb leaders in Islamabad. But there are other militant groups, more brutal, better armed, totally alien to the valley, totally under the control of Pakistan and willing agents of its wishes. It could be difficult to institute a cease-fire if they did not observe it. But these are somewhat limited calculations. Going beyond them is the broader fact that the recent cease-fire, though limited and short-lived, was the product of a deeper and wider change which has been taking place in Kashmir, and it lifted this change to a much higher level.

The change first stirred when other Kashmiris also began to ask themselves what a former Chief Minister of Jammu and Kashmir, Mir Qasim, asked the Pakistan High Commissioner in Delhi more than a decade ago : Will Pakistan be able to persuade or militarily push India out of Kashmir ?. When the High Commissioner gave the obvious answer, "No", Qasim asked why then was Pakistan stoking a militancy which was slowly decimating a whole generation of Kashmiris. To this there was no answer of course, and the question continued to ripple out into every widening circles.

It took a few years for the real potency of this question to come home to me. The governments in New Delhi and Srinagar agreed to my request to let me meet Imran Rahi in prison. He had been arrested when he was the deputy commander of the Mujahideen, and had been described to me by other separatists as a fine example of a Kashmiri militant in the prime of youth. He had been in jail for some time with Ayesha Erabi, of the Dukhtran-e-Milat, who had fully lived up to her reputation as a fiery speaker when I had met her earlier. But encouraged by Rahi's patently sincere and honest personality, I put Qasim's question to him. He reflected for a minute and then replied with quiet admission that the gun had led them nowhere, and they must think again. I asked him whether I could quote him on that by name, which I did later, and he agreed because, as he explained, there were others also, in the same jail and outside, who were veering round to the same view. He was released soon after, and he never went back to the gun.

I narrate this background only because it is a measure of the change which has come about in the valley. Such questions are no longer being asked and answered in privacy but are candidly debated in the press. This is partly the result of the success of counter-insurgency but has been pushed up by recent events. The Kargil operation was one among them, which showed people that even when Pakistan did resort to a military effort and caught Indian troops on the wrong foot and off guard and on very difficult terrain, it was forced to pull back. The diplomatic reverse Pakistan suffered soon after was also not lost on Kashmiris. But a bigger change was wrought by the cease-fire episode, which not only placed on the table what was once unthinkable but made it the centre of an alternative agenda.

A wave of relief swept through the valley when the Kashmir wing of the Hizbul Mujahideen announced a unilateral three-month cease fire with no conditions attached, and the Union government made a prompt and very positive response. Hope suffered a setback when New Delhi tripped in an irrelevant controversy over the question whether the talks would be within or outside the Constitution; only what comes out of them may have to be. But it recovered when Prime Minister Vajpayee declared unambiguously that the government side would not walk away from talks if the Hizb suggested changes in the Constitution. And it recovered further when Kashmir saw the contrast between the warm approval the Hizb won when it announced the cease-fire, and the widespread criticism Pakistan earned, including some from its own people, when it pressured Salahudin into killing the cease-fire.

There are many examples of the change of discourse in Kashmir. But I will give only a few. In its issues since mid-August, an Urdu weekly of Srinagar, long respected for its frankness, has published many reflections of it. A brief headline summed it first : "Talks failed, but the change is there." It blamed "vested interests" which, it said, had "sabotaged the process" and blunted the expectation that "hope of peace was neither a daydream nor an illusion."

In subsequent issues it made deeper analyses, and the most significant came from a senior Hizbul commander, commander Masood, in defence of the cease-fire. It extolled "the indigenous character" of the Hizb and thus deprecated its control by "an outside group" in violation of an earlier agreement to put the Hizb in charge at "the diplomatic and political levels" also, in addition to its "militant activities". It criticised those who, in their "campaign for conquering the world" exposed "the Kashmiri people" to "torture and killings". It noted that "the ray of hope" they might have seen in Kargil "got drowned in Washington." The cease-fire, it said, was Hizb's "own decision" and was announced "to show the real face of the movement" and its "true nature", and it would have won the support of "other militant outfits" also but for the "hasty" criticism by the Hurriyat, whom Masood criticised severely and on many counts. Masood also took on the Pakistan based Jehadi Council for removing Salahuddin as the leader of the Hizb after the announcement of the cease-fire, and for expelling the Hizb. He claimed if the Indian response had been sincere the Hizb would have waited not for three months but for three years.

None of this can be dismissed as water over the dam now, because it goes to the heart of what is the most basic question in Kashmir : Is Pakistan now making the mistake that India made in earlier decades, the mistake of not reading the valley right ? India made it when it misread the valley's, and indeed the whole state's desire for some autonomy as a cloak tailored by secessionists. Pakistan is now making it by expelling "the indigenous" Hizbul Mujahideen from the controlling council based in Pakistan and making it a pawn in the hands of the Pakistan-based Jamaat-I-Islami.

17

This Haste Will Haunt Us

Early, 2000

Whenever someone who has usually been eminently sensible does something which seems exactly the reverse, it is best to suspend judgement, because it is possible that there is more to the matter than has had time to meet your eye. However, suspension of judgement does not preclude examination of such evidence as exists for understanding events and reading their shadows. The present case in point is the way Prime Minister Vajpayee and Home Minister Advani on one side and Farooq Abdullah on the other handled the matter of the J&K state Autonomy Committee's Report, and what the consequences might be.

On June 30 several correspondents present at the Prime Minister's press conference on board his aircraft heard him say that the autonomy resolution passed by the J&K assembly was within the Constitution, and they so reported in the next morning's newspapers, in quotes. On July 2nd followed a "clarification". It said what the PM said was that the Report would be "considered in accordance with the Constitution." Both comments were unnecessary statements of the obvious. All powers of any state are, and can be , only as they are in the Constitution; they can be reduced or increased in (and only in) accordance with the Constitution and its amending procedures; any demand for changes can only be considered in accordance with the Constitution, and in that sense it is not outside the Constitution. The demand itself is unconstitutional only if made in an unconstitutional way, which a resolution by a state assembly is not, and if anything is conceded which is incompatible with the Constitution it is bound to be struck down in any case.

But the obvious was handled in a way which could only mean one of two things : either the Prime Minister was reported incompetently, or he was "rolled back", to recall a phrase often flung at Finance Minister Yashwant Sinha. Neither the credibility of the Prime Minister nor of the press gained any laurels. What this sequence did was only to heighten the contrast between what happened on the morning and the evening of July 4, and what the PM and the Home Minister had been saying until only a few days and hours earlier. Even in the in-flight press conference the PM said there was no mistrust between New Delhi and Srinagar, the Autonomy Report was not a "serious" development, and "this situation will be tackled with complete success".

The Home Minister went further on June 27. The Government of India will take a considered view on the autonomy resolution (and) ultimately it has to be decided by Parliament." Asked if other states would make similar demands, he replied "I do not think" while also adding that the National Democratic Alliance had received a mandate on the devolution of power to states, thus further allaying apprehensions that the Report had set a dangerous precedent. Similarly reassuring was his reported comment in London on June 22 that the Centre was not against autonomy, and "the J&K Assembly's views will be kept in mind when we consider the Report." This was after a 40-minute meeting between the PM and Farooq the preceding day. Of course the report itself had been in wide and public circulation for days.

Thanks to such views and their extensive reporting a mood of hope had spread through Kashmir which was summed up in a newspaper headline on July 1 which said "Fed up with war, Kashmiris forget azaadi, settle for autonomy", and a signed article by the paper's well known chief editor said "End game in the valley : Azaadi to

Autonomy." "There is a lot of room for give and take "he added in a highlighted passage. The mood of hope was justified because for years a credible report had been going the rounds that Mr PV Narasimha Rao, the longest ruling Prime Minister since Indira Gandhi, had said in 1995 that short of secession, "the sky was the limit" for autonomy. (In a conversation which was confidential at the time he had said this in the same words to the present writer also in the early 90s during a phase of one's considerable involvement in the Kashmir affair then and since.)

But what came to pass instead on July 4 was a startling anti-climax. At a single sitting that morning the Union cabinet rejected the Report "unanimously" and summarily. It was nothing like "this is acceptable", "that can be considered" "but that cannot be." The report was rejected in toto. Mr Advani announced "the government would not do anything" to bring the Report before Parliament though a private member could do what he might. This followed his statement on Doordarshan the pervious evening which can only be described as selective truth. He held up to the camera a copy of the text of the Indira Gandhi-Sheikh Abdullal Accord of November, 1974, and read a sentence from it which said "...provisions of the Constitution of India already applied to the State of Jammu and Kashmir without adaptation or modification are unalterable." But he said nothing about nine points which are going to matter much in the coming months :

First. The same Accord also says that the "adaptations and modifications" made in (numerous) provisions before applying them to the state can be "altered or repealed" on merits. Second. It also lists many other extensions of the Union's jurisdiction to the state after 1953 (that is after Sheikh Abdullah was arrested) which could be terminated, and the state's recommendations about them would be "sympathetically considered". Third. It promises "fullest consideration" to the views of the state in taking any steps, going beyond the acceeded subject of "defence", for protecting the safety and integrity of the state and of the Union. Fourth. The Accord is an extra-constitutional bilateral agreement between the Sheikh and Mrs Gandhi and open to change by mutual agreement between their successors. Fifth. The Centre is already committed, and proud to be, to devolve more powers to the states, including presumably J&K. Sixth. There is little difference between the quantum of powers the state may get under a practicable and exercisable autonomy and those it may get under a devolution which has now become practically irreversible all over the country and all the more so in J&K.

Seventh. If "give and take" had begun there would have been a good chance of consensus around the extension to the state of the jurisdictions of the Supreme Court, the Election Commission, and the Comptroller and Auditor General. As predicted to me, in the late 1950s as I recall, by Sadiq Sahib, the best Chief Minister the state has had, these jurisdictions are so popular with the average Kashmiri that no politician would have opposed the chance of a consensus on them. Eighth. Given that consensus, and the Supreme Court's new found power to protect " the basic structure" the state's essential interests in the Union and of the Union in the state would have been equally safe. And finally and most importantly, the issue on that fateful morning and evening of July 4 was not what was more constitutional but what was more conducive for a political climate, within the state and between it and New Delhi, which would nurture a consensus. Surely a sincere and open ended invitation to patient talks, not the abrupt and almost insulting rejection of the Report, which has sharply diminished the standing of the most outspoken Kashmiri defender of the state's accession to India and has encouraged some ambivalent leaders of the Hurriyat to push their oars into the newly troubled waters.

Who is responsible for this debacle ? Facts are scarce as yet. But the needle of speculation points to the two meetings the PM had just before the cabinet met, one with the BJP president , Mr Thakre, the other with Farooq Abdullah. Even while the PM and Home Minister were holding out uncommon hope, Thakre had already, on June 26, called upon people to reject the autonomy resolution, which he called "a retrograde step". Two days later the BJP General Secretary and party spokesman predicted rejection of the resolution by Parliament. It was the PM and HM that probably blinked, confronted with the false argument that other Indian states would prove to be dominoes. Farooq's failure was patent, and it must have soured his meeting with the PM. He had failed to keep his (reported) promise to the PM that the state assembly would only debate the Report, not adopt a resolution demanding its acceptance. Worse, while travelling up and down the country pledging his allegiance to the accession, and pleading hard for consensus in the rest of India, he could neither prevent anti-India venom in the assembly debate nor build a consensus among the people of the state, as shown by the demonstrations in Ladakh and Jammu. While trying to persuade the country that autonomy for the state was good for India he could not tell the two regions of the state what was in it for them. There is only a long way out of this mess, if there is one.

[illegible] [illegible] the M[illegible] [illegible] that prefaced
[illegible] [illegible] [illegible] [illegible] [illegible] [illegible] [illegible]
[illegible] [illegible] would [illegible] to [illegible] [illegible]
was [illegible] and if [illegible] the [illegible]

[illegible] had failed to [illegible] [illegible] to the [illegible]
that the ships [illegible] [illegible] [illegible] [illegible] [illegible]
[illegible] [illegible] [illegible] [illegible] [illegible] [illegible]
travelling up and down [illegible] [illegible] [illegible] allegiance
[illegible] [illegible] [illegible] [illegible] [illegible] for [illegible] [illegible]
[illegible] [illegible] [illegible] [illegible] [illegible] [illegible] [illegible]
[illegible] [illegible] [illegible] [illegible] [illegible] [illegible]
of the [illegible] [illegible] the [illegible] [illegible]
[illegible] [illegible] [illegible] [illegible] [illegible] that [illegible]
for [illegible] [illegible] [illegible] [illegible] [illegible] [illegible] [illegible]
[illegible] of the [illegible] [illegible] [illegible] them. There is [illegible]
and the [illegible] [illegible] [illegible] [illegible]

18

Returning to Lahore

Mid, 2000

Simple falsehood travels faster and goes farther than complex truth. India has experienced this problem for decades in its relations with many countries concerning its relations with Pakistan. For this reason India needs to be careful about some grand verbal flourishes in which Chief Executive Officer Parvez Musharraf indulged in the course of his recent diplomatic road show concerning the post-Kargil relations with India.

At the very start of our independence, India failed to counter the falsehood that the country was partitioned in 1947 on the basis of religion. It wasn't. It was partitioned as a result of territorial referendums which were held on the basis of the Indian Independence Act of the British Parliament, the constitutional basis of the termination of Britain's colonial power over South Asia. The Act made not a single reference to religion. That is why referendums were held, directly or indirectly, even in territories, such as the North-West Frontier Province, in which Muslims had always constituted ninety per cent or more of the population.

This was never a technical distinction without a difference. It was at the heart of the demographic problem that no matter how the lines of partition might be drawn there would always be more Muslims in what would remain

India than in what would become Pakistan. Their future would have been in peril in any partition mandated by religion.

Because this falsehood was allowed to hold the field for long enough, it bred a vicious trap. Pakistan got away with the falsehood that because India was partitioned on the basis of religion and because Kashmir was a Muslim majority province of the state of Jammu and Kashmir, it should have acceded to Pakistan. Dealing with constitutional complexities as lawyers would, India failed to convince the world that the Indian Independence Act had left it to the Maharaja of the State, as to the rulers of all the "princely" states, to decide whether the state should accede to India or Pakistan, whether the ruler and the population were of the same religion or not.

Nor, as a consequence, could India tell the world how, by marshalling an invasion of Kashmir by its tribal raiders and regulars, Pakistan precipitated the Maharaja's decision to accede to India while India had agreed to leave him free to decide his future as he chose and at his own pace.

A more serious and longer lasting trap followed soon afterwards, and it persists to this day. While India was branded for not carrying out a plebiscite as recommended in a UN resolution, India failed to bring it home to the world that, as recognised and recorded by the UN itself, it was Pakistan which frustrated the resolution by refusing to meet three obligations which it was required to meet before India could be asked to hold a plebiscite, and frustrated it for so long that, as again recorded by the United Nations, it ceased to be practicable.

It is true that the fault was not India's alone. The "Kashmir dispute" was still in its infancy when the world caught the high fever called the cold war. In that conflict many countries, notably led by the United States, considered India to be on the "other side" and Pakistan as a close ally. Therefore India could do nothing right and Pakistan nothing wrong in their eyes, and India lost the audience before it could carry conviction with anyone. But life is like that, and India has to be careful to ensure that deception, however simple to digest, does not again get the better of realities.

The reality is not, as CEO Musharraf claims it is, that Pakistan is willing to sit down "at any time with any one at any table." Or that he is willing to discuss anything with anyone "without any conditions." The first is the phrase he often used when he started his diplomatic tour, in South-East Asia, and the second when he landed in France. The reality is that he is trying to get away from the best table at which India and Pakistan have ever sat, with the best fare that has ever been served to them, and the tragedy is that, however unwittingly, India is playing into his hands, and this time it is doing so without even the extenuating circumstance of the cold war.

Ever since Prime Ministers Vajpayee and Nawaz Sharif met in Lahore, most countries which have taken an interest in peace in South Asia have expressed their appreciation of the "Lahore process", a phrase they use both for the negotiating process which the two Prime Ministers began with courage in that city, and for the two documents which came out of it. They have also advised both India and Pakistan to resume the process, and have done so with increasing earnestness since Pakistan's misadventure in Kargil.

Their reason is obvious. These are the two best documents in the whole history of "Kashmir diplomacy", whether in the UN or outside, in a bilateral or any other mode. The "process" required no midwives or mediators, was directly the product of the good sense displayed by both Prime Ministers, covered the agenda comprehensively, gave pride of place to the Kashmir dispute itself without denying due status to other issues between the two countries, and laid out a clear programme of work on them, clearer than in any other document so far. The documents are an improvement over the Simla Agreement because neither country signed them in the shadow of a military defeat, as Pakistan did at Simla.

It is unfortunate that the "process" has been overtaken by the bitterness and sense of betrayal felt in India – rightly — because of what has become known since the meeting in Lahore : that even while Nawaz Sharif was giving the hug of peace to Vajpayee and was negotiating the terms of the two blueprints for future peace, his generals, and particularly the future CEO, were planning and preparing for the bloody conflict which followed in Kargil. For this reason it is understandable why India is insisting on conditions which would ensure that such betrayals do not occur in future, but it would not be understandable if India also insisted, as it is doing to an avoidable extent, on conditions which have the makings of future traps for India.

India is prescribing four kinds of conditions before it can agree to resume the "Lahore process". Each is impractical as a condition for resumption, and together they can constitute a fourth trap, and perhaps also give the CEO an escape from the "Lahore process", which he has many reasons for disliking, and not least the reason that it is the handiwork of Nawaz Sharif.

First, India is insisting, as Prime Minister Vajpayee is quoted to have done in a speech at Anand on April 11, that "Pakistan must express regrets for the Kargil misadventure". Even (or particularly) defeated countries do not express regrets, we did not ask Pakistan to do so in any of the past conflicts or wars, not even after the Bangladesh war, in which Pakistan suffered its worst ever defeat. In any case regrets are not worth the paper they are written on. Those who express them are the first to forget them if they get the chance to do so. What matters is the price which the perpetrator is forced to pay for his misadventure, and Pakistan must not be allowed to forget that.

Second, in the same speech Mr Vajpayee also demanded that Pakistan must "desist from repeating it", that is the Kargil misadventure. In no country can today's government bind tomorrow's government to this conduct or that; nor can a third country bind it so. What India can do, and has come a long way closer to doing it, is to convince Pakistan that future misbehaviour by it will earn at least as harsh a response as it has done in the past, and India will insist on completing its response even if other countries requested it hold its hand. In other words here too India's own strength is a better guarantee than any assurance by a third country for ensuring better behaviour by Pakistan.

Third, Prime Minister Vajpayee also demanded that Pakistan "must learn to respect ... bilateral understandings." Of course it must, and a country's signatures to an agreement is supposed to be an affirmation of just such respect. But who can enforce this respect better than the other party to the "bilateral understanding" if it can make infringements of the understanding very expensive for the offending co-signatory to it ?

But the worst mistake is the fourth. In different forms of words India has been saying Pakistan must first discontinue its violent transgression across the LoC. Pakistan is denying it is making any. In this situation what is there to prevent the CEO from demanding, either on his own or through a friendly intermediary, that the UN or other international neutrals must actively patrol the LoC to see whether India's allegations are more correct or Pakistan's denials, and whether what India calls incursions from the other side are in fact only local insurgencies.

It would not be easy for India either to accept what would be a blatantly international intrusion or to reject it without appearing to be dragging its feet on the road back to the "Lahore process." That appearance would be expensive and unwise because it would put India at odds with those numerous countries, all of them strongly in favour of an early return to "Lahore", whom India has – rightly —thanked for their new and at last correct understanding of the realities of Kashmir, even if it has taken long to dawn on them. Once again the victim would become the accused and the offender the accuser.

The sanest and safest course for India would be to ensure early resumption of the process, and in the meantime to leave no one in any doubt that any violation by Pakistan of what India now calls conditions for resumption would be dealt with, promptly and fully.

PART-III
SURROUNDING SCENARIOS

Introduction

A Change of Drivers

While many Indians continue to fret over foreign "pressures" on India on the issue of Kashmir and relations with Pakistan, the issue itself has undergone a subtle change in the past few years. Perhaps the change is too subtle for some people to notice it, particularly some in Pakistan. But its meaning should be clear enough to sensitive Indians. The change is that while in the past more of this matter used to be decided by third countries, today more of it depends upon such decisions as India and Pakistan themselves may be able to take, though of course in taking them each also considers, as it should, the reactions of third countries.

A corresponding change has also taken place in the role the state of Jammu and Kashmir itself plays in the calculations of both India and Pakistan. In the past both countries could think – and did, however wrongly – that it was for them to decide the fate of the state, and each thought the people of the state would go along with the decision.. Today the state and its people are in the driving seat. They decided that even if Pakistan-based terrorists were outside their control as yet, it was time to disown Kashmiri terrorists to the point that they stood disarmed. They, not Delhi, decided that the state must be ruled in a way different from the way it had been ruled for nearly fifteen years by the favour of New Delhi.

Nevertheless, affairs which are foreign to this issue do impinge upon it to some extent, and Srinagar, New Delhi, and Islamabad do have to ponder over what happens in capitals other than these three. These affairs are the subject of Part III, particularly events in neighbouring Afghanistan, the Middle East, and in the all pervasive sphere of American politics. If the Indian and Kashmiri cries over the pain of terrorism have begun to be heard by the world it is because America has also felt that pain in its own bones. This explains both the impact of the choice India made even before terrorism blasted New York, that the emphasis in its approach to other countries would henceforth be more on the terrorist attacks on Kashmir than on Pakistan's aggression against India.

But there is also a downside to the increased international interest in India and the state, its concern over the danger of another war between India and Pakistan. While India's nuclear status has come to be more or less accepted by the world, the danger of use of nuclear weapons in was is still a worry.

1

India, Pakistan and the SAARC Debate

Early, 2002

Look at it whichever way you will, after the SAARC summit in Kathmandu. South Asia is faced with the task of squaring a circle. SAARC can do little for this region unless its two key members, India and Pakistan, cooperate fully in implementing its agenda. But if both are in it and stick to their present mutual animosities, SAARC can have no meaningful agenda. If Pakistan left it the organisation would lose its regional face. If India left it, SAARC would vanish.

This may seem a harsh comment to make on a session of SAARC which produced the best document it has ever produced on the (literally) burning issue of cross border terrorism. With the region facing the worst ever manifestations of this crime by one SAARC member against another, the Kathmandu summit has produced a ringing and comprehensive denunciation of it, and as signatories to the declaration all members are presumably bound by it. This is a signal achievement.

The same can be said about another aspect of the Kathmandu summit. What the region needs most is economic development. What has hindered it most is lack of economic cooperation between its key members. The cause of that in turn has been the chasm between the official economies of India and Pakistan. There is illegal trade between them through third countries. But while that fills private and black pockets in both countries, it deprives both governments of some of the revenues they need for all that can be legitimately called "development" as against wasteful expenditure by the respective money bags.

Much ice was broken on that count too at the Kathmandu summit. India had been pushing for it all along, but in a low key so that its motives may not be misunderstood, by Pakistan in particular. But at Kathmandu General Musharraf, with apparent purposefulness, moved virtually into the driver's seat. He pleaded for a fast forward rush by SAARC towards SAPTA and SAFTA, the two main projects for cooperation among the SAARC countries in trade and commerce which Pakistan had previously hindered the most. So that too should count as a strong plus point for the Kathmandu summit.

But that does not lift the shadow which relations between India and Pakistan have cast on South Asia. Beyond declarations and speeches lies the huge barrier of the intentions of each towards the other. A good example is the long standing and deplorable fact that in violation of international agreements to which both countries are signatories, Pakistan refuses to reciprocate India's gesture in giving MFN status to India.

There is no force in Pakistan's argument that armed with MFN status India would flood Pakistan with its manufactures and ruin Pakistan's indigenous industries. India has made two offers in response to this argument. The first is that Pakistan should allow India to compete in its market at least with regard to those items which it imports from other countries. The second is that both countries can exchange negative lists, that is enumerating those items which either does not wish to import from the other, but for the rest give genuine MFN status to each other. Pakistan has responded to neither offer.

But for such obstructiveness, SAARC would move ahead

sufficiently fast in certain fields to encourage progress in other fields as well, because there is no intrinsic difficulty about regional cooperation in South Asia. During the 1970s I was living in South-East Asia and closely followed the development of ASEAN. In the next decade I had the opportunity of following the progress of SAARC through corresponding stages, and I found the latter to be progressing faster. But then that was a time when, for his own reasons (mainly his ambitions about Afghanistan and further north and west) the Pakistan leader, General Zia, was interested in peace on his eastern flank and was cultivating India for that reason. This only shows that when mutual interests and mutual perceptions thereof coincide, progress can be as fast in South Asia as in any other region.

Does it mean then that SAARC in general and India in particular must resign themselves to a Pakistani veto on the whole organisation ? Upto a point yes, but not entirely. An alternative could be that those SAARC members that are genuinely interested should go ahead as fast as they can with regional and bilateral cooperation, demonstrate the benefits thereof to those who are holding back still, and then to let the latter come in at their own pace. Easier said than done, true. But there are good examples of success. India and Bhutan have benefited immensely from cooperative use of river water resources. So would have cooperation between India and Nepal if the Indo-Bhutanese model had been demonstrated earlier. But it has its uses even now. For example, in the development of untapped rivers in Nepal and the gas resources of Bangladesh. But the process will be slow, will require a lot of patience, even more willingness to see the other's point of view (which India has often failed to do) and even then the gains will be only a fraction of what they could if Pakistan also chose to see the light of reason.

sufficiently fast to [illegible] progress in [illegible] as well, because there is no immediate difficulty about regional cooperation in South Asia. Before the [illegible] in South-East Asia and closely followed the development of ASEAN in the first decade [illegible] and the [illegible] following the emergence of SAARC. Through concept [illegible], and hence the [illegible] that was a [illegible] for [illegible] about [illegible] and [illegible] under [illegible] [illegible] as to [illegible]

Consequently, the [illegible] in general, and [illegible] [illegible]

2

India, America, and Terrorism

Late, 2001

India's foreign policy can be faulted on many genuine counts. Therefore spurious ones do not have to be invented by those who wish to throw stones at it. Yet the mills of invention are hard at work, at times even on issues of the greatest importance for India. A major example surfaced in mid-summer this year. Another is unfolding right now. Both may be forgotten soon enough, or at least fall into place. But the danger continues that while we chase phantoms in this fashion some real thieves my slip through. Of that too there are current examples.

In late May and early June this year noted Indian commentators accused India of jumping up in support of NMD, a pet project of President Bush, with which the eager new broom was trying to write his name into history while still trying to learn his way around the White House. The project causes great concern to Russia because it is completely incompatible with the ABM treaty between Moscow and Washington, which Russia regards as the indispensable cornerstone of international security architecture in the nuclear age. India too has the same position as Russia about ABM and NMD, and has laid it out in more than one official and publicly available document, some dating back to the start of the Bush presidency, some more recent.

Therefore, some Indian commentaries which implied

warm Indian support for NMD embarrassed Indo-Russian relations. That by itself would not have been reason enough for the commentaries to hide any facts based on reliable documentation which questioned the official Indian position. But that was not the case. Commentaries were, and remain, backed only by some tortuous interpretations of stray Indian references, including imaginative reports of where it all began, a telephonic conversation between the Indian Foreign Secretary, Chokila Iyer, and the Security Advisor to President Bush, Condelezza Rice, at a time when both were new to their respective jobs. But such was the impact of the commentaries, at that time and since, that references to an enthusiastic Indian welcome to NMD keep cropping up even now despite a public statement by Ms Rice that Ms Iyer had expressed no support for the NMD project, and despite official and published documents which show that India has always opposed NMD as inadmissible under ABM, which neither signatory can set aside unilaterally.

Closer to today are commentaries which say that India first pledged "total support" to America's "crusade" against terrorism, and since then has been busy backing away from it. Neither part of the comment is correct. In his very first message to President Bush after the terrorist attack on New York on September 11, Prime Minister Vajpayee said India was "ready to cooperate with you in the investigations into this crime and to strengthen our partnership in leading international efforts to ensure that terrorism never succeeds again." Next day the Foreign and Defence Minister, Mr Jaswant Singh, added that the Prime Minister's offer was "unambiguous and unconditional". There is no conflict between the Prime Minister's statement and Mr Jaswant Singh's elaboration, nor between either of them and any of India's subsequent statements and actions, nor any backing away from the PM's offer, as far as it went, of cooperation in "investigations" and in ensuring that "terrorism does not succeed again". There has only been further elucidation of the Indian position, for example that Islam should not be identified with terrorism or with "the terrorist agenda of fomenting hatred and division in society on communal lines", and that there must be a reaching out to Muslim majority countries like Iran, and that there should be "a concert of democracies", and that the actions taken should be "legal" or as approved by the United Nations.

In fact what is conspicuous about the policy positions taken by India in both these cases, in the matter of NMD and India's support for the fight against terrorism, is the speed with which policies were formulated in the face of sudden and new developments, and the consistency with which they were followed up with such compatible actions and statements as were possible. That some opposition parties remained unconvinced critics may be consistent with their view of the role of opposition parties. But unsubstantiated criticism is not consistent with anyone's view of the role of impartial criticism and comment.

More noticeable is the lack of comment, as far as one is aware, on two serious disclosures of the role of President Clinton which became public in the midst of the turmoil over terrorism.

In recent years, and particularly during the second half of Clinton's second presidency, America showed a better understanding of India's problem with the terrorism practiced against it from across the border with Pakistan. In the field of foreign policy also America began to say in public that it would not intervene in the matter of Kashmir unless invited to do so by both India and Pakistan, and it urged each country not to use violence against the other to change the present status of the dividing line in Jammu and Kashmir. It also began to admit that armed groups were operating in Kashmir which were coming in from Pakistan and were not receiving, as claimed by Pakistan, only moral and material aid from that country. Yet it now transpires that in a matter as recent and as important as the conflict

[illegible] of [illegible] there [illegible]
President of the United States, however, [illegible] direct responsibility on the governments of Latin America. The [illegible] which have not [illegible] close to the [illegible] upon which Chilean [illegible] had [illegible]. They agreed that [illegible] of Latin America [illegible] domestic [illegible] would [illegible] their [illegible] America.

Once [illegible] these points [illegible] September 11 has there been greater need than now [illegible] India to remain [illegible] and [illegible] of India, so long as the [illegible] upon the [illegible] committed [illegible] against [illegible] come [illegible] two opinions [illegible] each [illegible] what kind [illegible] what kind of [illegible] them.

3

Beyond Clones of Osama

Late, 2001

It is an irony of our times that the greatest military alliance put together against the kind of terrorism that has swept across the world from Afghanistan has America at its head and Pakistan as its forward base. It is ironic because between them these two countries are the father and mother of exactly this type of terrorism.

America planted the deadly seed when, after single mindedly flooding Afghanistan with weapons of destruction in order to drive the Soviet army out, it simply walked away. It took not the slightest precaution to see that this arsenal would not be turned upon the neighbours of Afghanistan and upon the Afghan people. The seed then produced what became the largest and most deadly army ever to serve a government which, at that time, was recognised by hardly any country. This is the army that was then adopted by General Zia, the most successful military dictator of Pakistan, who nurtured it into a weapon of his dream of Nizam-e-Mustafa, a republic of Islamic fundmentalism stretching form the Indian border deep into the Volga country of Russia via Checheniya and Tatarstan.. It is a further twist of irony that it is the progeny of this very dream which invented the worst destruction ever to be rained upon the world's most powerful country, and which – another twist – had also claimed Pakistan to be its most allied ally.

If one recalls these painful facts it is not out of any heartless disregard of the tragedy of New York. One does it for three reasons. First, to remind America that zealous but shortsighted pursuit of any single objective, however attractive it may seem at the time, can have dangerous off-springs if the attendant and downstream consequences are not kept in view.. Second, to remind all of us that we should abandon strategies which would end up cloning new Osamas out of new Talibans. Third, to point out that the only option before us is not to reduce Afghanistan to an even more tragic rubble of history than it has been already by its own rulers, the Taliban, ably assisted by Pakistan. A much higher option for the world is to begin with a new future for Afghanistan and to go on to burying all that remains of the nightmare of the cold war.

Take the first reason first. America has rightly decided to take up the job in hand by phases. It wishes to concentrate first on those who perpetrated the tragedy. As it does so, America merits the support of all countries, including India, without quibbling over unnecessary differences between allowing American planes or soldiers being allowed only to transit through India or also to be assisted in some way. But as America deals with the first phase it must not forfeit the future, as Ronald Reagan did.

Reagan fought the anti-Soviet war in a way which only armed America's future enemies. In focussing so exclusively on the destruction of what he called the "evil empire" without sparing a thought for subsequent dispensations, he left the door open for those who have been hitting America ever since and have now reduced the heart of New York to a wasteland. Whether the Soviet Union fell more because of Reagan's hatred of it or because of some other causes, the weapons of hatred he chose have taken a heavy toll of America and of Pakistan, in addition of course to what they have done to Afghanistan.

Second, the present perpetrators of the present tragedy

are the products of a process. All the pain of dealing with the products will go in vain if the process continues. A new generation of fanatics will take over from where the old generation left off, and to the new generation America will be all the more Satanic because it eliminated the old. The process will produce the new generation in the same way that it produced the old, beginning with what Pakistan did about Kashmir. Defeated in war, Pakistan chose fanatical Islamists as new soldiers against Kashmir, and it turned to a willing Afghanistan as the recruiting ground. It gave all help, covert, overt, military, financial, to organise and arm those who were proud to describe themselves as the soldiers of Islam though in the eyes of other Muslims they were betrayers of the best traditions of the faith. A cascade of Talibanisation then began which flooded Afghanistan first, then large parts of Pakistan, and then other parts of the Islamic world.

Three kinds of signs that the process may continue have surfaced already. In the first place influential people in the anti-terrorism alliance are indicating already, as Blair did in a TV interview on September 29, that the Taliban could be allowed to remain in power in Afghanistan if it handed over Osama and banned his organisation, Al Qaida. That by itself would not prevent other individuals and organisations from replacing them. In the second place, America might go along with Blair if Pakistan demands that as the price for allowing use of its territory. In the third place, in the name of resisting interference in the internal affairs of Afghanistan, the Pakistan Foreign Minister has publicly announced his opposition to any assistance by anyone to the Northern Alliance, which is the only credible internal opposition to the Taliban regime. Pakistan – and President Bush — cannot have forgotten of course that, quite contrary to Pakistan's present opposition to "interference", it was only with massive assistance by and through Pakistan that the Taliban drove out the Rabbani government from Kabul, which was the widely recognised government of Afghanistan at that time and which was, and remains, a member of the United Nations.

The alternative to these dire scenarios is that America should accept what many countries are urging, that the fight against terrorism should be conducted under the authority and flag of the United Nations. It will then get more willing support from more countries, as many of them have indicated already. Notably Russia, and the CIS neighbours of the Northern Alliance. With support from so many on so many fronts, the Taliban (and those who continue to support it) will become more isolated and less able to exploit the anti-American sentiment which exists in many Muslim majority countries. Their resistance will end faster, and Afghanistan will be spared, firstly, the agony of a prolonged war, and secondly severe attacks by air, which are naturally more indiscriminate but can become more necessary in the absence of many-sided ground action.

There can also then be a more far reaching and more constructive consequence — a closer convergence between American and Russian concerns, actions and aims, bringing the curtain down on the cold war. For some months now Russia has been urging that either it should be admitted into NATO as a full member or that NATO should be replaced by a new security consortium which embraces the whole of Europe, east and west. To that it has now added that a common fight against all manifestations of terrorism, wherever and in whatever form, offers the chance of a strategic convergence between Europe, Russia, and America. The Pakistan President also conceded on October 1 that the days of the Taliban are now numbered. All the more imminent, then, is the challenge and the opportunity for a strategic convergence on a post-Taliban dispensation in Afghanistan as the first step for a convergence with a broader aim.

4

The Other Battle for Kabul

Late, 2001

In the past few days a play about Afghanistan has been on view in and out of Kabul. It is a miniature version of two much bigger dramas which were acted out in 1944-45. A common theme runs through the three, that large scale political calculations can displace military calculations.

In the closing phase of the Second World War in Europe, the Red Army broke through the German border and raced on to Berlin. This worried the Allied armies which were at that time busy in western and southern Germany, and they also wheeled around to head for Hitler's capital, because each side wanted to make sure it would not be left out of the city which had become the citadel of Europe. The first shots were then fired in what soon became "The Struggle for Europe", to quote the title of Chester Wilmot's fascinating book, published in 1951. That struggle is only now dying down (if it is) half a century later.

On the other side of the globe, American armies had practically brought Japan to its knees by that time, and according to many historians of that war complete victory could have been won with a few more weeks of conventional war. But a political task had to be accomplished first : to make a field trial of the ultimate weapon so that all future contenders for power may also be warned off. So a million Japanese lives and the cities of Hiroshima and Nagasaki had to be sacrificed, and one particular contender was later named by Churchill quite clearly in his Fulton speech when he said " matters must be brought to a head with the Soviet Union before they too have the nuclear bomb."

What has all that to do with tiny little Kabul ? A lot, because the implications of the Kabul drama ripple out into the politics of Pakistan and Central Asia, into the role of the United Nations, into the honeymoon between America and Russia, and into the future oil map of the world. All the strands of this drama go round and round Kabul, tying up the military battle for Kabul with the political calculations of other battles for it.

Since one of America's top aims has been to see the Taliban government thrown out of Kabul, it should have been happy when the Northern Alliance swept down from the mountains and got ready to do just that. But America directed it not to enter Kabul. Why ? An answer for a time was that the directive was only a sop for Pakistan, which was nervous about the anti-Taliban Alliance ruling a next door neighbour.

But that answer faded when America initiated serious moves in the UN to block the formation of a government by the Alliance. Its probable reason : America has invested in new found friends in Uzbekistan, while the fighting arm of the Alliance is inspired by the charisma of the quintessential Tajik, the late Ahmad Shah Masood. The Uzbeks have drawn closer to America because lately they have been suspicious of Russia, while the Tajik force is backed by Russia (and behind that by India).

America would also have calculated that once the victorious Alliance came to power in Kabul it would take the bit between its teeth, or else the same tribal disorder would recur as had forced the American oil giant, Unocol to write off the millions of dollars it had invested in a pipeline through Afghanistan to the new oil wealth discovered in Central Asia. So why not opt immediately for a pliable government under the aging Pushtoon king, Zahir Shah, strengthen it with European and American backing, and give it legitimacy by putting it in the Afghan seat in the UN General Assembly ?

But these calculations have run straight into some political realities, local, national, international. The present occupant of the UN seat has been there for two decades, representing a country which is a full fledged member of the UN, and recognised to be so by many countries. He continued to occupy it when his government had lost most of the country and its capital, Kabul. How is he to be replaced now when his government has regained most of the country and the capital, and when an assertive, vigilant and veto-wielding Russia has already declared that the Alliance is the legitimate government, and the Alliance has questioned the right of any country to send troops into Afghanistan without its permission ?.

If a tussle ensues now between Russia and America within the UN on this issue, it will only further heat up a very large and friction prone issue which has already cropped up, involving competing Russian and American interests in the Afghanistan region. This concerns the vast new sources of oil which have been lately discovered in Central Asia. The sources themselves are in clearly defined national jurisdictions about which there is no dispute. But American and other Western companies have quickly built financial stakes around them, and are now being advised to fence out Russia and Iran.

They are planning and building a system of pipelines in an East-West land corridor which runs north of Iran, south of Russia, mostly through Central Asian states, across the Caspian Sea and Black Sea, and thus into the lucrative oil markets of Turkey and Europe. There should be nothing wrong with that, except that one of the aims of the system is being clearly stated to be what is bound to arouse tempers in Moscow, Teheran and Riyadh. This aim has been only mildly stated by the Caspian Studies Programme at Harvard, which says America should loosen "OPEC tentacles" and resist "political blackmail" by Saudi

Arabia by getting more Caspian oil, and also to "by-pass Russia and Iran" through the new pipelines.

But a study at the Woodrow Wilson Centre is much more explicit, and offensive towards Moscow and Teheran. In a report published in September it says "The United States has important political and strategic stakes in the Caspian region" but the countries of the region would "remain vulnerable to Russia's hegemonic impulses" and therefore they must build "close, substantive relations with the West... independent of their huge neighbours to the north and south", that is Russia and Iran.. Their "dependence on Russian pipelines would be dangerous". Similarly it says "Kazhakastan would be ill-advised to entrust its energy security to Iran." To reinforce the point it adds "a major role for American companies" had "contained Iran's regional influence at a time when that country's policies were particularly anti-American."

These rivalries of course are not new. They ante-date the jostling for power which is now going on in Kabul for control over Afghanistan, and they began separately and from different causes. But they interact very closely with the long term interests of Russia and America in this region, and are therefore very relevant to the latest Afghan drama. In what manner and how far they will influence the power balance in the Caspian corridor or to the south or north of it may not be known as yet. But they are fuelling and are being fuelled by the current military and political battle for Afghanistan.

The battle against the Taliban has given America a promising military presence right next to Afghanistan, in Uzbekistan, which it is seeking to enlarge and prolong. On the political plane, the hope of the Northern Alliance, now re-named United Front, that it will become the new ruler of Afghanistan has now been matched by moves for a "provisional authority" to take over the country under the UN flag and in the name of law and order. If the Alliance could not be stopped at the gates of Kabul, why not confine it within Kabul ?

5

The Visit and After

Early, 2000

Clinton's visit to India was good. It was made even better by the contrast with what happened in Pakistan. But there might be snakes and ladders ahead. India must be ready to side-step the former and climb up the latter. The Indo-American future may then be better than it has ever been.

Clinton did not sign, seal and deliver much that was both specific and significant. What was specific was not great. The agreements signed and deals struck were modest. Of course there was the "vision" statement. But apart from being flawed in some respects as critics have pointed out, it was more a promissory note than a commitment, a cocktail of good intentions distilled out of the unprecedented "feel good factor" which Clinton unleashed with the triumph of his diplomacy through personality and turn of phrase.

But the immediate result was remarkable. Prospects that had seemed very unlikely in the past few years began to look very probable in the next few. The ground got ploughed with goodwill as it has never been before. More seeds got sown than in any earlier season. The climate changed as with a wand. Indian public opinion was purged of its habitual mistrust of America and the American purged of the once infamous "tilt" towards Pakistan. At least for the time being.

The transformation was at least as remarkable as in Indian feelings for Britain during the late 1940s and early 1950s. Or even for Pakistan during Rajiv Gandhi's brief duet with Benazir Bhutto or Vajpayee's bus yatra to Lahore. These comparisons may seem ominous, because they show how hopes based on moods can perish. But it seems more likely that they will bear some fruit this time, though the Clinton presidency might miss them. Take a few probabilities:

- America may reject India's "nuclear doctrine" in its fullness but a more "minimum" Indian deterrent will no longer provoke the "roll back and eliminate" hectoring in which Madeline Albright indulged even a few days ago before Clinton began his discovery of India.
- The painstakingly gentlemanly labours of Jaswant Singh and Strobe Talbot will remain a persuasive precedent for the Indo-US dialogues which, commendably, the "vision statement" has written into the joint agenda of the two countries.
- India and America may (one hopes) never become strategic partners, but Indian interests have become and will remain a factor in American (as indeed in Russian and Chinese) calculations about security dynamics in Asia, not only in South Asia.
- Future pictures of South Asian geo-politics, even if drawn in America, will no longer mistake the Pakistani scale for the Indian scale.
- The image of a cerebral India will stand alongside, and perhaps taller than, the (somewhat unrealistic) image of an India full of a vast consumerist middle class.

Some changes have occurred in the more limited South Asian picture as well, and they are likely to endure into the post-Clinton America as well if India continues to abjure obduracy. For instance :

- The ghost of the UN resolutions on Kashmir, which were killed by Pakistan, not India (a fact admitted by the UN also before its brain was frozen by the cold war) will never hover over an Indo-US banquet even if Pakistan sneaked in.
- On the other hand bilateral Indo-Pakistan talks will remain the first option for any significant third country which may choose to advise either country, or both, on this matter.
- The Lahore initiative, which means both the Declaration and the joint statement signed by the Foreign Secretaries of the two countries, can no longer be brushed aside unilaterally by Pakistan because of General Musharraf's allergy to them.
- There will be wider acceptance in India now of Clinton's position that while "we will not and cannot mediate" he could help to "restore the promise and process of Lahore."
- Pakistan will now find it very difficult to trigger direct mediation by any major third party by threatening that otherwise it will ignite nuclear fires in South Asia. The world will accept it from the American President, if it did not from India, that Pakistan is using the threat to blackmail third countries into intervening in Kashmir on its behalf.
- Whether India or Pakistan like it or not, the Line of Control has become the first choice of most third countries as the basis for a settlement unless the two countries can bilaterally come up with an alternative.

In his broadcast to the *people*, not the government of Pakistan, Clinton warned Musharraf against trying "to redraw borders with blood." Thus he further elevated the status of the Line of Control. In his tight faced reply on TV Musharraf tried to by-pass this warning by claiming LoC was only a line, not a border. The world will not believe this now, nor should Pakistan forget what happened to it when it tried to change the "line" with blood.

Echoing the words India has used often, Clinton said Pakistan too "must create conditions that will allow the dialogue to succeed." That hurt, and Musharraf claimed dialogue to succeed." That hurt, and Musharraf claimed India had "de-educated" Clinton.

But the Clinton visit, the "vision", and their fall-out also have traps which India must negotiate with the greatest care. They are the "snakes".

First, Clinton, America, and the world in general will judge India adversely if it is seen to be dragging its feet on the road back to Lahore. India should therefore not impose any undefinable or unverifiable "conditions" for restoration of "the promise and process of Lahore." Such as the condition that "jehad" and "violence" must stop. What is "jehad", by whose definition, and whose violence against whom ? Such terms are a minefield of definitional problems and should not be used as "conditions."

The two Lahore documents are on the table, and both countries stand committed to them. If either country wants to discuss what they entail or wants any changes in them it must come to the table. But the agreed texts must be the starting point of what may follow. They cannot be rubbished, as the Pakistan foreign minister once tried to do. That must remain India's only and consistent "condition."

Second, New Delhi's – and Srinagar's – handling of the situation within J&K continues to be deplorable, and very damaging for its case both at bilateral and international fora. This must improve, and as soon as possible. Otherwise it will undermine all the potential that awaits India in all arenas — bilateral, regional, Asian global – in terms of the "vision statement."

Third, there are phrases, concepts, suggestions in the statement itself which must be unpacked with the greatest care. Otherwise they may spring very inconvenient surprises upon us later on, as India undertakes the burdens of "partnership"—strategic, economic, or diplomatic—before it gains the strength to reap its benefits.

6

What Can November 7 Mean for India?

Late, 2000

Ever since it became independent, India has always watched American presidential elections with interest. The reason is obvious : America's role in affairs of close concern to India. When the Quit India Movement launched by Mahatma Gandhi seemed likely to undermine the war effort in India, which was Britain's main supply base for soldiers and war material in the eastern, south-eastern, and middle eastern theaters, America argued strongly with Britain to win Indian support. Guided as much by its own struggles against British colonial rule, and its democratic traditions, as by concern for successful pursuit of the war in Asia, America urged Britain to announce immediately that India would get independence, if not during then at least very soon after the war. America thus became the most popular country in India.

This continued into the later 1940s, when America cautioned Britain against the tendency on the part of the British Foreign and Home offices to question the accession of Jammu and Kashmir to India. The British position seemed strange to Indians because it was Britain which had given to the rulers of the princely states the right to decide the future of the relations of their states with India and Pakistan, and it was the ruler of J&K who had decided in favour of acceding to India. But then Britain produced an argument which silenced America.

Britain argued that the issue was not the rights and wrongs of the accession. The issue was whether the post-war interests of the Anglo-American alliance would be better served by J&K becoming a part of India or of Pakistan. Kashmir lay on the best route to the soft underbelly of the future enemy, the Soviet Union, and the vulnerable eastern flank of China, at that time a staunch and potentially powerful ally of the Soviet Union. Pakistan was willing to become a total ally of the West while India would prefer to remain nonaligned. Therefore the Kashmir route would be safer in the hands of Pakistan than of India. America became a zealous convert to this point of view and later the flag carrier of Pakistan's position on Kashmir.

These events were soon to become the cause of a deep chill in Indo-American relations. To these were soon added two more. One, the United States refused to sell some fighter aircraft to India and the technology for making them in India later; and two, it rejected India's request for aid to build a steel plant, on the ground that the plant would be in the public and not in the private sector. India's alienation from America became so great then, and was to remain so for so long, that whenever an American presidential election came along India's official and unofficial America watchers searched earnestly for any signs to see which party would be less inimical to India.

It is a sign of the more relaxed relations between the two countries now that any differences there might be regarding India between the two main parties in the American presidential election – and there *appear* to be no significant ones anyhow have not generated much Indian interest in the current presidential election. Reflecting this lack of interest, and partly explaining it, is a chatty comment sent to me by Stephen Cohen, who is among the half a dozen Americans who, knowing America very well of course, have also maintained a close interest in India and Pakistan. He writes "The question 'would Bush or Gore be good for South Asia/India/Pakistan' can't be answered without heavy qualification, because regional developments (meaning in South Asia) have not figured in this election at all, and foreign policy only marginally....The days are long over when Democrats were more 'pro-Indian' and Republicans more 'pro-Pakistan'. The difference this time is likely to be the degree of interest and activity in South Asia that one or the other might pursue ; the Republican platform has a lengthy paragraph on the importance of strengthening ties with India (but notes that the US should not allow relations with Pakistan to suffer), the Democratic platform puts South Asia in the context of various global problems, such as non-proliferation and human rights concerns. However platforms count for little after the election, when policies tend to be driven by events ..." And then, in another comment he adds "My wife (Roberta) and I cannot decide whom to vote for..." But since both parties are well disposed towards India, anxiety does not spark much concern in India the outcome of the contest.

These appearances are not misleading at all, but they do not reflect the total reality. There are significant differences between the two parties, and though "events" will certainly do much to shape the country's and the government's policies, respective attitudes, which are well rooted in habits, will also play a significant part. Cohen confirms as much when he says the Democrats used to be more "pro-India" and the Republicans more "pro-Pakistan". There are differences between them on several issues which could affect India's interests.

For instance the differences between them on a missile defence system, or what is popularly called " star wars", which can put a shield over a country or a theatre to protect it against nuclear missiles. Its biggest supporter was Ronald Reagan, the most gung-ho president of America outside fictional caricatures and cartoons, and the most outstanding Republican since the end of World War II. The phrase and the fact of "star wars" was his contribution to the American agenda, and he lavished funds upon it with such abundance that the Soviet Union, forced into a competition which it did not want and could not afford, was sent into financial ruin. In that sense Reagan, to whom the Soviet Union was "the evil empire", won the star war without firing a missile at the enemy.

The Democrats first moderated this programme's huge appetite for funds, then took it off the front burner, and under Gore it would recede further because he has made a bigger commitment than any president to socially beneficial programmes, which also need a huge of amount of money if they are to have much meaning. The Republicans on the other hand would be loath to slow it down too much, having criticised Clinton for doing so even to the small extent he did. Besides, the Republicans have much closer links than the Democrats with the high profile end of the arms industry, as indeed with the uppermost strata of the corporate world in general

The fate of the star wars programme can affect India indirectly. If America went ahead with it in a big way, neither Russia nor China would sleep in peace. Russia has the technology for an answer, but not the resources for developing and deploying it. But China is much richer, and together they can marry the technology and resources required for at least a modest but sufficient reply. It could consist of, firstly, enough number of missiles between them to make sure that some at least would get through, and secondly, enough protective cover for each of them to take care of the most important targets of their respective countries.

If that happened, India would have to re-think its whole nuclear equation with China. The present equation is based on the Indian assumption that even though India might not be able to catch up with China in the number of nuclear missiles that the two countries possess already or might possess in future, India would at least have enough to pose a counter threat to some critical targets in China, not to many but to a sufficient number for China to think twice before deciding whether what it might gain by attacking India would be worth the risk of even a limited retaliation by India. In that sense even a dozen or so Indian nuclear capable missiles are sometimes mentioned, for example by the late General Sunderji, as being a sufficient deterrent against a rationally calculated attack by China. But if China had a sufficient nuclear shield in the sky to cover all of its critical targets, then how many more missiles would India need in order to maintain its deterrent capability ? And would India be able to afford as many ? That would re-start the whole Indian debate about the economics of nuclear deterrence.

An "event" that could become what Cohen called a "drive" to push this star war scenario – in which the defender's computers would send up a missile to intercept and destroy what they sense as the approach of an attacking missile – is the on-going clash between China's ambition to unite Taiwan with mainland China, and Taiwan's hope of becoming independent. Gore's Democrats and Bush's Republicans are both committed to the defence of Taiwan, but the Republicans much more stridently so. The Democrats, under Clinton, have made quite an effort, with some success, for relaxed relations with China. It is not clear that the Republicans would do that too. If they did not, how would China react ? In addition to being rich it is again close to a Russia which is recovering politically under Putin, continues to be a giant in both nuclear fire power and technology, and is strapped only for cash. Which way would this "event drive" the combination ?

There is also another India-related China dimension to November 7. Both parties are wary about China's future intentions, but the Republicans much more so and also much less willing to disarm China with appeasement. The Republicans under Nixon opened America's first channel to China, through Pakistan, but that was done to detach China from the Soviet Union. How would they react if China and Russia now got much closer together, and what would that do to their Indian policy ? There is a sneaking scenario among the policy planners of both parties in which India, if it can fulfil its potential, is seen as a counter-poise to China, as both saw it in the wake of the India-China conflict in 1962. But here again the scenario is closer to the Republican than to the Democratic heart. A Republican in the White House could also become another driving event. How would India handle that event, seeing how close Russia is to India also ? What would happen to India's present stance towards China, seeing that at present India is more than willing to improve relations with China as well ?

Take another event. Since the nuclear tests by India, Clinton's top people have engaged India intensely and for long over India's ambitions. As a result America has softened its nuclear agenda with India. From demanding that India roll back to become non-clear again, America has changed to urging India not to let its ambitions exceed its needs, and also be more realistic in assessing how many missiles its needs, of what range, and how ready for instant use. Washington has also lifted many of the sanctions it imposed after the tests. But the Republican attitude continues to be harder. On the other hand America under a Republican President is much less likely than under a Democrat to sign CTBT and another SALT agreement with Russia, and if America does not sign the Treaty it is not going to be able to coerce India into doing so.

There is yet another "event", but more related to France and Russia than to China. France is keen to enter the Indian market for nuclear energy plants and technology. But France is a member of the western dominated "suppliers' group", which has prohibited its members from cooperating even in the civilian nuclear energy field with any country which does not accept, and India does not, full international inspection of all its nuclear installations, including those it may develop on its own. France has tried to find a way round that prohibition but is not known to have succeed so far.

In the meantime Putin has signed up India as a market for Russian plants and technology, and has assured India that it will not bend to any such prohibition. How it will manage to resist the western pressure is not very clear. Russia did ultimately get round American restrictions on Russia supplying cryogenic engines and technology to India. But firstly that was at a price India had to pay in terms of delays and costs as India, with Russian help, developed indigenous engines. Secondly, that event happened when a Democratic was in the White House. Will it happen again with a Republican there ? It remains to be seen. But it also remains to be seen whether the Republicans will bend to the pressure which is bound to come from the American nuclear industry that it should not be left out of the Indian market when the Russians are able to get in, and the French will surely try harder then to get in too.

So it is obvious that even though Gore and Bush are Tweedledum and Tweedledee in domestic politics and on many foreign policy issues too, India's interests could possibly be affected in many matters of some concern to it whether dee gets in or dum. But the one issue on which they will not be affected by the American voters' choice on November 7 is India's relations with Pakistan, or for that matter on the Kashmir question. There is no noticeable difference between the two parties on these issues now even though one was supposed to be more "pro-India" once and the other "pro-Pakistan". Each, when in office, will fine tune its policies as the situation develops on the ground on South Asia. But India needs to take note that both will desire resumption of the long interrupted Indo-Pakistan dialogue, and if India is not to fall foul of the next incumbent in the White House, whether Republican or Democrat, it should either agree to resume the dialogue or give better reasons for not doing so than it has given so far. India has talked in the past with military rulers in Islamabad and cannot convincingly refuse to do so now. Nor can India realistically demand that all intrusions from Pakistan across the Line of Control must stop first. Who is to verify whether they have, and what would India say if Pakistan proposed that international observers should be invited to inspect the border regime on both sides of the Line ? India has so far been opposed to any further form of "internationalisation".

7

The Muslim Cause

It is wrong to take a distorted view of Islam or of Muslims. Or of any religion or community. To do so deliberately is vile, and an invitation to trouble. Unfortunately, this happens most when it is most important to avoid it. That is in times of tension and anxiety, when the broad brush of prejudice is most often used to paint those we disagree with. When the issue is big, prejudice gets a bigger brush. The prejudices of some then become the prism through which whole communities begin to see other communities. But before adding another word, I must express solid sympathy with Farooqui's complaint about the media in his article "Clash of stereotypes" (*HT*, 30. 10.01). With him I fear that many a media room is cluttered with misperceptions or worse. Professional values fly out of the window when figures of revenue and circulation come in by the door.

But the issue here is not why "someone" should be "stereotyped" merely because, as Farooqui's article implies, he "adhere(s) to religious rituals fanatically ". The issue is whether most people in a community agree that all religions have the right to their rituals in a multi-religious and multi-cultural world (or country). If some agree but many don't then the rational few get stereotyped along with the dominant trend. Farooqui shares this failing.

He speaks of "the real precursors of the Taliban State"

and among them he names "Mussolini's Italy, Franco's Spain, Salazar's Portugal, Tojo's Japan, Ian Smith's Rhodesia, the apartheid State of South Africa, and above all Hitler's Germany." All of them are blots on history books. But in all of them the rational spoke out loud and clear until they were silenced, and spoke out again when they could. But can it be claimed that at least in the countries they rule and where they have the trumpet voice of the majority, Muslims have spoken out against "the Taliban State"? He has rightly said the Taliban are "as ruthless and undemocratic in their pursuit of absolute power as the Nazis were." True. But from how many Muslim platforms in Muslim majority countries have the Taliban been denounced as such ? From how many has Pakistan been cautioned against building them up, or Saudi Arabia against financing their training grounds ? It was a well publicised fact that Pakistan was rearing the Taliban behind the shield of Islam as the future sword of its imperial ambition. Yet so little was said against that by recognised platforms of the faith that the Taliban became a stereotype of the faithful.

This collective silence has become a towering prism through which the collectivity is seen by others despite the many Muslims who, like Farooqui, "have dedicated themselves to combating communal politics.." The dominant trend, attitudinal or "on a specific issue", becomes the rule in the eyes of the observer and the exceptions get identified with the rule. Those on the other side of the prism return the compliment, and misperceptions multiply. That is why the Taliban, and what they have done to Afghanistan, have done to some other countries also, and threaten to do to still others, figure so much in the current debate in many countries, and also in Farooqui's response to the article by Vir Sanghvi (October 14).

Farooqui is right in deploring that a wrong view of Muslims is spreading among non-Muslims. But this ailment has its causes. They should be faced and cured, not brushed under a carpet of side issues and definitions. The main cause is the process by which a dominant trend becomes the prism of perception. The dark events enacted on September 11 are a good illustration. No responsible person has accused any Muslim community or country of condoning those events, because most of the authentic Muslim voices have condemned them. A positive image of the Muslim has thus stood out clearly on *that* issue. But his pre-September 11 image was far from clear and positive, because he was ambivalent about the image of the Taliban as the ugly Muslim. If a "wrong view of Muslims" has grown—and it certainly has–then the main reason is that on the whole they are generally seen to have condoned the Taliban phenomenon and many are seen to have even idealised it.

Individual Muslims have spoken, with courage and eloquence, even about the role being played by the Imam of Jama Masjid, to whom Farooqui also refers, and he must have seen Mushirul Hassan's open letter to the Imam. But are they candles in the wind or "a broad based political campaign" which Farooqui says "liberal Muslims" are waging in "the cause of secularism"? Or are they more like footnotes written in fine print, which can elucidate or qualify a point in the thesis to which they are appended but which cannot replace the thesis? As for example the scholarly annotations which seek to explain the Quranic meaning of Islam or of Jehad. That meaning is wonderful. But the Taliban reject the footnotes. The real life jehadi does not even read them. "The campaign" is worthy of support, and must be continued despite the mirrors of the media failing to reflect it. But can it demolish the deceiving prism? The answer is negative yet. Hence the danger of the "Hindu backlash" in Vir Sanghvi's article.

What can make the answer less negative ? In the reality of mass politics, images are made by momentous issues, and these should not be left to the mercy of "the rabble rousers" who, as Farooqui rightly laments, "make it to the headlines." Such issues constitute occasions when "articles/rejoinders" strike a cord and the media cannot but "care to have a look." The world would have paid attention if the distortions of Islam which were being manufactured in Afghanistan with Pakistani technology had been exposed in time in and by the countries which profess truer Islam. That opportunity is now slipping. Another, very relevant to India, was lost almost a decade ago.

Some years ago someone approached me in the respected name of "Ali Mian" (the late Maulana Abul Hasan Ali Nadwi) to support and join an organisation, Muslim by name and predominantly so by composition, in a campaign for secular solutions to the Babri Masjid and Kashmir issues. I joined it, both in public appearances and private discussions, but soon found myself running into a devious game. What was accepted in private discussion was frustrated in public debate.

In private the organisers accepted my plea that the while many Hindus, like me, questioned the wisdom of New Delhi's approaches on many Kashmir related issues, they rejected the argument heard from Pakistan that since the Kashmir valley had a Muslim majority it belonged to Pakistan because India had been partitioned on the basis of religion. The organisers agreed Pakistan was falsifying history, and that it could have dangerous consequences. But they always suffocated a public debate on that issue, while I believed that such a public position by a noted Muslim organisation on such an urgent issue would help to remove misperceptions about the stand taken on it by Indian Muslims. This difference persisted, and I left the organisation.

But this is only a minor illustration of a major phenomenon : that just as misperceptions get forged in the public mind in a heated debate, as since September 11, they are best removed when clear stands are taken on matters of urgent concern. An Islamic plea on behalf of

Kashmir can sharpen the profile of the faith in the mind of the faithful, and perhaps make some of them more fanatical. But it will do little good to the cause of Kashmir or the cause of Islam. Or to the Muslim cause, which Farooqui rightly describes as the cause of "the vast majority of ordinary Muslims who go about their daily business", however fanatically they may "adhere to their religious rituals."

What Next?

In most of the preceding pages it has been argued that Pakistan has been steadily losing the advantage it had over India for almost forty years because of its strategic geographical location in respect of west and central Asia and because of its diplomatic location in the context of the cold war. This advantage reached its peak in the 1980s when Pakistan's usefulness to America, both in geographical and diplomatic terms, was at its height. Since then it has been losing this advantage because of the end of cold war, the collapse of the Soviet Union, the improvement in America's direct relations with China, the improvement in India's relations with the United States and China, India's greater self-reliance in economic terms and the resulting increase in its relations with much of the western world, particularly with the United States, as the latter's interest in economic diplomacy has increased and need for scoring cold war points against India as an "ally" of the former Soviet Union has declined. Above all, America now needs Pakistan much less because it now has its own direct access to as well as military basis in Central Asia and diplomatic presence in Afghanistan.

On the other hand as the universal concern over "terrorism", or over what is loosely called "Islamic fundamentalism", has increased, India's relations with many countries which have suffered at the hands of similar forces have improved because in varying degrees all of them see India as a fellow victim of these same forces. This change has even improved their understanding of India's case on

Kashmir. At no time in the past have so many countries shown so much more sympathy for India's case on the attack by Pakistan-based jehadi forces on Kashmir and on the rest of India. This change has been further improved by the results of the latest elections in the state of Jammu and Kashmir, and in Pakistan. Whereas the elections in Kashmir have shown significant gains there by secular and democratic parties which either support the state's' accession to India or do not oppose it, the elections in Pakistan have a further strengthened those same "fundamentalist" forces there which so many countries in the west, and Russia, are trying to fight in Afghanistan, Iraq and elsewhere in crucial countries in West Asia.

But some events have also occurred in the recent past which appear to point the other way. While it acknowledges that cross border terrorism against India from the side of Pakistan has not ended, the United States has increased its support to Pakistan lately, including some in arms which Pakistan is bound to use against India if it can invent an opportunity for doing so. At the same time Pakistan has also adopted a more threatening posture towards India. In the first place Pakistan continues to support terrorist activities against India by bands based in Pakistan, arguing that it had never promised to stop such support permanently. In the second place the Pakistan President, General Musharraf, has held out the threat that he might try another Kargil type attack on India, and he has not been called to order by the United States. It has been left to the Indian Prime Minister, Mr Vajpayee, to do the needful, which he did in the appropriate way of warning Pakistan that if it tries to attack India yet another time it should be ready to face yet another defeat, because Pakistan has lost every war it has launched against India, including the latest, in Kargil.

These recent events raise the question whether the present author is wrong in his view that Pakistan has been steadily losing its leverage against India. The answer is a firm NO, for the following reasons. First, what is true does not become false simply because someone refuses to admit that it is true. Nor does reality vanish because someone turns a blind eye to it. And in analysing how Pakistan has been losing its leverage the author has expressed no hope that Musharraf or someone else has or will learn the correct lesson from the change. Second, it has not been argued anywhere by the author that the United States has completely got over its frequently displayed habit of subordinating its long term interests to some short term and short sighted goal.

What has been argued on the other hand is that whereas during the long decades of the cold war America's long term interests in an important area were anchored upon Pakistan's strategic location, now they are not. This change is of such magnitude that even President Bush cannot shut his eyes to it for any length of time. He might subordinate it for some time to the immediate compulsion he faces to produce as many Al Qaida bodies as he can before the next Presidential election in America, and in that task he certainly needs as much help as can get from Pakistan. But such electoral or other ephemeral considerations are not the stuff of which long term strategic policies are made. When America's long term interests come to the fore in its policy councils as they must, sooner rather than later, the scene changes that have taken place in Kashmir, India, and Pakistan, will play their part. One sign of the change will be that neither the West in general nor America in particular will be as willing as they were during the cold war to twist the Kashmir case against India and in favour of Pakistan.

But in the interregnum India faces the delicate task of weighing its own long term and short term interests with a cool and unhurried mind. For example over America's keenness to enlist the support of an Indian peace keeping force in Iraq. There are strong reasons why India should give a positive response but equally strong reasons why the response should be cautious and subject to certain conditions, particularly the need for a UN mandate. Hitherto India has handled the dilemma well and calmly. But an example more immediately relevant to the theme of this book relates to Jammu and Kashmir. It is likely that as soon as America's preoccupation with Iraq and Palestine eases, it will start paying more attention to South Asia and the Kashmir question. In doing so it will try to give some comfort to Pakistan as a reward for Pakistan's willingness to continue its services to America. One form that the comfort will take will be to be more forthcoming in starting talks with Pakistan and ease the condition upon which India has so far insisted, that there can be no talks until the ongoing cross border terrorism against India ends and Pakistan destroys the bases from which terrorism is guided and supported by Pakistan.

At that point India will have to choose between the embarrassment of easing that condition and the twin risks of appearing to be obdurate and inviting still stronger pressure from America and others. The material risk will not be great either way, the diplomatic risk might be and that can have material consequences. The hard but obvious answer is in four parts. First, to get the best terms it can for the modalities of the talks. For example that they will be strictly bilateral, between India and Pakistan, with no third parties either sitting by their sides or looking over their shoulders, and that they will not begin at the top but may rise to the summit after careful preparation at lower levels. Second, about the subject of the talks. They must begin with the agenda which the two parties have already agreed upon in the form of the much acclaimed Lahore documents, which have a pride of place for Kashmir, security and nuclear safety, but also include a number of other important subjects. Of course once the talks begin on this basis they can include any changes in or additions to or substitutes for these documents that the two countries may agree upon. Third, if Pakistan cannot assure complete end to terrorism before the talks begin or during the talks, India must retain the right to retaliate and respond in any manner it may see fit to any act of terrorism against it. Fourth, any agreements that may result must be self-contained and final, with no overseeing role for any third party, and subject only to any such regime for international agreements as may exist at that time.

In addition to these conditions for the talks, there is a condition surrounding the talks which the governments and the peoples of the two countries must create : that should clashes and casualties occur during the talks or other difficulties arise, the public outcry should not be such as may drown serious consideration of such delicate issues.

A more delicate issue of mood which must be managed relates to personality equations within the government of Jammu and Kashmir, and political equations between Srinagar and New Delhi. This issue might seem easier to manage because it lies within India's and the state's domestic jurisdiction but it remains vulnerable to Pakistan's ability to manipulate the temperature of both kinds of equations because of its control over the terrorists. Both kinds can be affected by the actions and reactions which may follow if Pakistan steps up terrorist activities and New Delhi and Srinagar step up counter-measures. Political issues which genuinely lie within the domestic jurisdiction of the state can also then begin to play the role of the spoiler.

First the personality equations within the government of the state. Thanks to the quality of leadership asserted by Mrs Gandhi during a critical phase in Kashmir after the victory of the alliance between the Congress and the state's People's Democratic Party, the state Congress agreed to let the PDP leader, Mufti Mohammad Sayeed, be the first Chief Minister in the new government in the state. But that agreement will end in 2005, and then it will be the turn of the Congress to hold that office for the rest of the term of the alliance government. It is possible, even probable, that the changeover will not create any major difficulty. But some friction cannot be ruled out, seeing how much of it there was prior to the state Congress leaders agreeing to withdraw in favour of the Mufti. More worrisome will be the use to which this friction might be put by two kinds of opponents of the alliance. First, the out and out opponents of the state's accession to India, and second those like the state's National Conference which supports the accession but is bitter over losing its decades old tenure in office.

If this disturbs the state's politics in any serious way, Pakistan will be tempted to disturb it further in two ways. First through the Hurriyat, which continues to operate in both above the ground politics and as an underground agency with links in Pakistan. Second, through stepped up direct and violent activity by the terrorists. Obviously the government will have to come down hard on that. The Congress might not object to that very much because it knows from its own past how hard the choices can be when terrorism calls the shots and some innocent Kashmiris become the victims. But the PDP will squirm because one of its election pledges was that it will impart a "human touch" to the government.

It is against this background that the Government of India will have to fine tune its course if the United States and others not only urged New Delhi to resume talks with Pakistan but also to similarly engage with the political secessionists in the state. In that situation New Delhi might be tempted to go slow with its current round of active political talks with all overground Kashmiris in order to see how it might need to trim them to accommodate what it can. But this would be a mistake. Much wiser would it be to continue with the dual policy it has been following so far, and which now has much greater support in Kashmir than before, that while Indo-Pakistan talks are a matter of external relations, talks between New Delhi and Srinagar are a domestic matter of both, and must remain so, until the time comes for them to figure in Indo-Pakistan talks.

APPENDIX

The Lahore Declaration

The following is the text of the Lahore Declaration signed by the Prime Minister, Mr. A. B. Vajpayee, and the Pakistan Prime Minister, Mr. Nawaz Sharif, in Lahore on Sunday:

The Prime Ministers of the Republic of India and the Islamic Republic of Pakistan:

Sharing a vision of peace and stability between their countries, and of progress and prosperity for their peoples;

Convinced that durable peace and development of harmonious relations and friendly cooperation will serve the vital interests of the peoples of the two countries, enabling them to devote their energies for a better future;

Recognising that the nuclear dimension of the security environment of the two countries adds to their responsibility for avoidance of conflict between the two countries;

Committed to the principles and purposes of the Charter of the United Nations, and the universally accepted principles of peaceful co-existence;

Reiterating the determination of both countries to implementing the Simla Agreement in letter and spirit;

Committed to the objective of universal nuclear disarmament and non-proliferation;

Convinced of the importance of mutually agreed confidence building measures for improving the security environment;

Recalling their agreement of 23rd September, 1998, that an environment of peace and security is in the supreme national interest of both sides and that the resolution of all outstanding issues, including Jammu and Kashmir, is essential for this purpose;

Have agreed that their respective Governments:

- shall intensify their efforts to resolve all issues, including the issue of Jammu and Kashmir.
- shall refrain from intervention and interference in each other's internal affairs.
- shall intensify their composite and integrated dialogue process for an early and positive outcome of the agreed bilateral agenda.
- shall take immediate steps for reducing the risk of accidental or unauthorised use of nuclear weapons and discuss concepts and doctrines with a view to elaborating measures for confidence building in the nuclear and conventional fields, aimed at prevention of conflict.
- reaffirm their commitment to the goals and objectives of SAARC and to concert their efforts towards the realisation of the SAARC vision for the year 2000 and beyond with a view to promoting the welfare of the peoples of South Asia and to improve their quality of life through accelerated economic growth, social progress and cultural development.
- reaffirm their condemnation of terrorism in all its forms and manifestations and their determination to combat this menace.
- shall promote and protect all human rights and fundamental freedoms.

- Signed at Lahore on the 21st day of February 1999.

Atal Behari Vajpayee - Prime Minister of the Republic of India, Muhammad Nawaz Sharif - Prime Minister of the Islamic Republic of Pakistan.

Joint Statement

The following is the text of the Joint Statement issued at the end of the Prime Minister, Mr. A.B. Vajpayee's visit to Lahore:

In response to an invitation by the Prime Minister of Pakistan, Mr. Muhammad Nawaz Sharif, the Prime Minister of India, Shri Atal Behari Vajpayee, visited Pakistan from 20-21 February, 1999, on the inaugural run of the Delhi-Lahore bus service.

2. The Prime Minister of Pakistan received the Indian Prime Minister at the Wagah border on 20th February 1999. A banquet in honour of the Indian Prime Minister and his delegation was hosted by the Prime Minister of Pakistan at Lahore Fort, on the same evening. Prime Minister, Atal Behari Vajpayee, visited Minar-e-Pakistan, Mausoleum of Allama Iqabal, Gurudawara Dera Sahib and Samadhi of Maharaja Ranjeet Singh. On 21st February, a civic reception was held in honour of the visiting Prime Minister at the Governor's House.

3. The two leaders held discussions on the entire range of bilateral relations, regional cooperation within SAARC, and issues of international concern. They decided that:

(a) The two Foreign Ministers will meet periodically to discuss all issues of mutual concern, including nuclear related issues.

(b) The two sides shall undertake consultations on WTO related issues with a view to coordinating their respective positions.

(c) The two sides shall determine areas of cooperation in Information Technology, in particular for tackling the problems of Y2K.

(d) The two sides will hold consultations with a view to further liberalising the visa and travel regime.

(e) The two sides shall appoint a two member committee at ministerial level to examine humanitarian issues relating to Civilian detainees and missing POWs.

4. They expressed satisfaction on the commencement of a Bus Service between Lahore and New Delhi, the release of fishermen and civilian detainees and the renewal of contacts in the field of sports.

5. Pursuant to the directive given by the two Prime Ministers, the Foreign Secretaries of Pakistan and India signed a Memorandum of Understanding on 21st February 1999, identifying measures aimed at promoting an environment of peace and security between the two countries.

6. The two Prime Ministers signed the Lahore Declaration embodying their shared vision of peace and stability between their countries and of progress and prosperity for their peoples.

7. Prime Minister, Atal Behari Vajpayee extended an invitation to Prime Minister, Muhammad Nawaz Sharif, to visit India on mutually convenient dates.

8. Prime Minister, Atal Behari Vajpayee, thanked Prime Minister, Muhammad Nawaz Sharif, for the warm welcome and gracious hospitality extended to him and members of his delegation and for the excellent arrangements made for his visit.

Lahore,
February 21, 1999.

Memorandum of Understanding

The following is the text of the Memorandum of Understanding signed by the Foreign Secretary, Mr. K. Raghunath, and the Pakistan Foreign Secretary, Mr. Shamshad Ahmad, in Lahore on Sunday:

The Foreign Secretaries of India and Pakistan:-

Reaffirming the continued commitment of their respective governments to the principles and purposes of the U.N. Charter;

Reiterating the determination of both countries to implementing the Shimla Agreement in letter and spirit;

Guided by the agreement between their Prime Ministers of 23rd September 1998 that an environment of peace and security is in the supreme national interest of both sides and that resolution of all outstanding issues, including Jammu and Kashmir, is essential for this purpose;

Pursuant to the directive given by their respective Prime Ministers in Lahore, to adopt measures for promoting a stable environment of peace, and security between the two countries;

Have on this day, agreed to the following:-

1. The two sides shall engage in bilateral consultations on security concepts, and nuclear doctrines, with a view to developing measures for confidence building in the nuclear and conventional fields, aimed at avoidance of

conflict.

2. The two sides undertake to provide each other with advance notification in respect of ballistic missile flight tests, and shall conclude a bilateral agreement in this regard.

3. The two sides are fully committed to undertaking national measures to reducing the risks of accidential or unauthorised use of nuclear weapons under their respective control. The two sides further undertake to notify each, other immediately in the event of any accidential, unauthorised or unexplained incident that could create the risk of a fallout with adverse consequences for both sides, or an outbreak of a nuclear war between the two countries, as well as to adopt measures aimed at diminishing the possibility of such actions, or such incidents being misinterpreted by the other. The two side shall identify/establish the appropriate communication mechanism for this purpose.

4. The two sides shall continue to abide by their respective unilateral moratorium on conducting further nuclear test explosions unless either side, in exercise of its national sovereignty decides that extraordinary events have jeopardised its supreme interests.

5. The two sides shall conclude an agreement on prevention of incidents at sea in order to ensure safety of navigation by naval vessels, and aircraft belonging to the two sides.

6. The two sides shall periodically review the implementation of existing Confidence Building Measures (CBMs) and where necessary, set up appropriate consultative mechanisms to monitor and ensure effective implementation of these CBMs.

7. The two sides shall undertake a review of the existing communication links (e.g., between the respective Directors-General, Military Operations) with a view to

upgrading and improving these links, and to provide for fail-safe and secure communications.

8. The two sides shall engage in bilateral consultations on security, disarmament and non-proliferation issues within the context of negotiations on these issues in multilateral fora.

Where required, the technical details of the above measures will be worked out by experts of the two sides in meetings to be held on mutually agreed dates, before mid 1999, with a view to reaching bilateral agreements.

Done at Lahore on 21st February 1999 in the presence of Prime Minister of India, Mr. Atal Behari Vajpayee, and Prime Minister of Pakistan, Mr. Muhammad Nawaz Sharif.

(K. Raghunath)
Foreign Secretary of the Republic of India
(Shamshad Ahmad)
Foreign Secretary of the Islamic Republic of Pakistan

1997 Indian-Pakistani Foreign Secretary-level Talks

Joint Statement

1. The Foreign Secretaries of Pakistan and India, Mr. Shamshad Ahmad and Shri Salman Haider met in Islamabad on 19-23 June, 1997.

2. During his stay in Islamabad, the Indian Foreign Secretary was received by the President of Pakistan and the Prime Minister of Pakistan. The Indian Foreign Secretary also called on the Foreign Minister Mr. Gohar Ayub Khan.

3. As decided at their meeting in New Delhi in March 1997 and as directed by their respective Prime Ministers, the Foreign Secretaries of India and Pakistan continued their wide-ranging and comprehensive dialogue on all outstanding issues between the two countries with each side elaborating its respective position. The discussions were held in a cordial and constructive atmosphere. It was also agreed that both sides would take all possible steps to prevent hostile propaganda and provocative actions against each other.

4. With the objective of promoting a friendly and harmonious relationship between Pakistan and India, the Foreign Secretaries have agreed as follows :-

   (i) to address all outstanding issues of concern to both sides including, inter alias:

(a) Peace and security, including CBMs
(b) Jammu and Kashmir
(c) Siachen
(d) Wullar Barrage Project / Tulbul Navigation Project
(e) Sir Creek
(f) Terrorism and drug-trafficking
(g) Economic and Commercial Cooperation
(h) Promotion of friendly exchanges in various fields

(ii) to set up a mechanism, including working groups at appropriate levels, to address all these issues in an integrated manner. The issues at (a) and (b) above will be dealt with at the level of Foreign Secretaries who will also coordinate and monitor the progress of work of all the working groups.

5. The two Foreign Secretaries also had a preliminary exchange of views on the composition of the working groups and their methodology. It was decided to continue the consideration of this matter through diplomatic channels.

6. The next round of Foreign Secretary-level talks will take place in New Delhi in September 1997.

Press Statement by the Foreign Secretary of Pakistan

We had started work in New Delhi on identifying the outstanding issues between India and Pakistan and on devising a mechanism to address them purposefully. This aspect of our work has been completed and the result is before you in the shape of the joint statement.

I am happy to state that we have successfully completed the first stage of the task entrusted to us by our two Prime Ministers. As you will note the two sides have agreed to address all outstanding issues with a view to achieving the goal of good neighbourly and cooperative relations.

We hope that the mechanism on which we have agreed will initiate progress towards the settlement of all outstanding issues listed in the joint statement. On our part, we will continue the dialogue with sincerity and serious purpose.

We have no illusions about the complexity of the work ahead of us. It is important for both sides now to take steps to create conditions conducive to make the process purposeful and result-oreinted.

Press Statement by Foreign Secretary of India

The Joint Statement, which is with you, really speaks for itself. In our view, it provides the basis for comprehensive, constructive and sustained dialogue between India and Pakistan. It is the result of four days of intensive discussions. These have been part of the process initiated in Delhi in keeping with the directions given by the two Prime Ministers. The Joint Statement identifies and lists out a number of subjects. It also sets out a mechanism for dialogue including Working Groups. Preliminary discussions have also taken place on constituting the Working Groups and their modalities. These aspects will be discussed further in Delhi when the Foreign Secretaries meet in September. It is our purpose that the dialogue leads to establishment of trust, friendship and cooperation between the two countries.

Joint Press Statement

Pursuant to the decision of the Prime Ministers of Pakistan and India to exchange fishing boats and crew presently in the custody of either side, the matter was discussed in detail during the Foreign Secretary level talks. The two sides have now verified 26 Pakistani boats and 195 crew and 25 Indian boats and 194 crew. It has been decided to release them by July 15, 1997. It has also been decided that other boats and crew will be released as and when identified.

[New Delhi]
[June 23, 1997]

Index

J

K

W

Z